PRESENTED TO:

_____

PRESENTED BY:

_____

DATE:

_____

GOD'S
ROAD MAP
FOR MOMS

Bordon and Winters

WARNER
Faith ®

New York Boston Nashville

Concept: Bordon and Winters

Project Writing and Compilation: Molly Detweiler, Deborah Webb, Shanna Gregor, and Betsy Williams in association with SnapdragonGroup℠ Editorial Services

Warner Faith
Time Warner Book Group
1271 Avenue of the Americas, New York, NY 10020
Visit our Web site at www.warnerfaith.com

Printed in the United States of America
First Warner Books Edition: April 2006

ISBN:0-446-57889-4

LCCN: 2005937103

INTRODUCTION

The road of motherhood, as you know if you've been walking on it for very long, has many unmarked intersections and cross streets. Not only that, but it weaves up, down, and around through all types of landscapes and terrains. The journey provides moments of breathtaking beauty and others of abject fear. There are dark stretches, detours, and of course, the danger of getting lost. What's a traveler to do? Happily, God has provided a road map—the Bible—to help us avoid dangerous and time-consuming delays and keep us on the path to our desired destination.

In *God's Road Map for Moms*, we have mined the Bible for wisdom and understanding that will be helpful on your journey. We've included Scriptures on the topics you may have questions about and laid them out in an A-Z format so they will be simple for you to find and follow. We've also added to each topic an illustrative Bible story or practical devotional to help you on your way. Finally, we've provided heartfelt prayers and letters that express some of the thoughts and feelings God has revealed in His Word that we hope will inspire and encourage.

We hope you will find all you need as you prepare your children for the time when they will leave your side and begin their own journey down the road of life.

The Publishers

Contents

Ambition

We . . . have as our ambition, whether at home or absent,
to be pleasing to Him.

2 CORINTHIANS 5:9 NASB

Make it your ambition to lead a quiet life, to mind your own
business and to work with your hands, just as we told you,
so that your daily life may win the respect of outsiders and so that
you will not be dependent on anybody.

1 THESSALONIANS 4:11-12

The apostle Paul wrote, "I make it my ambition to
proclaim the good news."

ROMANS 15:20 NRSV

The desires of good people lead straight to the best,
but wicked ambition ends in angry frustration.

PROVERBS 11:23 MSG

Jesus said, "If any of you wants to be my follower,
you must put aside your selfish ambition, shoulder your cross daily,
and follow me."

LUKE 9:23 NLT

Wherever there is jealousy and selfish ambition,
there you will find disorder and every kind of evil.

JAMES 3:16 NLT

IN MY FATHER'S HOUSE

"Where do you think He is?" Mary asked, whirling around to face Joseph who stood looking over the landscape.

She was frantic. They had assumed that Jesus was in the family caravan headed back to Nazareth when they left Jerusalem that morning.

"I don't know, Mary," Joseph answered, shielding his eyes from the setting sun. "We'll have to head back in the morning and find out."

"We can't wait till morning!" A knot was swelling in her throat, damming up tears that threatened to burst through. "It's his first trip to the city; what's a young boy to do there without his family?"

"He's a competent young man, Mary," Joseph assured. The experience at the Jerusalem feast had impacted Jesus much more deeply than they had anticipated. He had seemed somehow distant, even detached.

"I'm sure you're right," she responded, rubbing her throbbing temples.

"We'll head back tomorrow," he promised. "There is nothing we can do now but pray."

When Mary found Jesus in the temple two days later, she burst into tears. Relieved at the sight of Him, she ran to wrap Him in her arms, crying, "Son! Where have you been? Your father and I have been so worried."

"Why were you searching for me?" He asked. "Didn't you know I had to be in my Father's house?" (Luke 2:49).

But they did not understand what He meant. His aspirations were higher than their minds could grasp.

As a mom, you might not always understand your child's ambitions simply because you would prefer to anchor him to yours. If you listen with your heart, however, the chances are greater that your child will open his to you.

Celebration

Encourage each other and build each other up,
just as you are already doing.
1 THESSALONIANS 5:11 NLT

The father of the prodigal son said, "Let's have a feast
and celebrate. For this son of mine was dead and is alive again;
he was lost and is found." So they began to celebrate.
LUKE 15:23-24

Accept one another, then, just as Christ accepted you,
in order to bring praise to God.
ROMANS 15:7

The Lord, your God, is in your midst,
a warrior who gives victory;
he will rejoice over you with gladness,
he will renew you in his love;
he will exult over you with loud singing.
ZEPHANIAH 3:17 NRSV

Rejoice with those who rejoice. . . . Live in harmony with one
another; do not be haughty, . . . never be conceited.
Repay no one evil for evil, but take thought for what is noble
in the sight of all. If possible, so far as it depends upon you,
live peaceably with all.
ROMANS 12:15-18 RSV

CAUSE FOR REJOICING

When you are able to look beyond the differences you have with your child over hair, style of dress, friends, and curfew—issues about which you often disagree—you'll find there are many things about which you can rejoice.

Observing your child for the course of one week, take note of the following:

- daily routine
- habits (desirable and undesirable)
- interests (sports, books, hobbies, magazines)
- appreciation of nature (animals, plants, solar system)
- relationships with people (siblings, friends, neighbors)
- attention to detail
- visionary tendencies
- early signs of expertise

Under the heading "Reasons to Celebrate," make a list of the things you observe and let that be your guide for some creative expressions of your love. Here are some suggestions:

Monday—Put a special treat for breakfast on the cereal shelf.

Tuesday—Leave a cool new hairbrush or brand of toothpaste on the bathroom counter.

Wednesday—Record a special sporting event on television for your child or pick up the latest fashion magazine.

Thursday—Put a goldfish in your child's bathroom for a touch of companionship or buy a hanging basket for his or her bedroom window.

Friday—Leave a card on your child's pillow expressing your appreciation for the friend, son, daughter, grandchild, etc. he or she is.

The idea is to celebrate your child the way your Heavenly Father celebrates you. He knows all about your flaws and yet He loves and celebrates you every day. Go and do likewise.

Challenges

Despite all these things, overwhelming victory is
ours through Christ, who loved us.
ROMANS 8:37 NLT

I can do everything with the help of Christ who
gives me the strength I need.
PHILIPPIANS 4:13 NLT

Consider it a sheer gift, friends, when tests and challenges come at
you from all sides. You know that under pressure, your faith-life is
forced into the open and shows its true colors. So don't try to get
out of anything prematurely. Let it do its work so you become
mature and well-developed, not deficient in any way.
JAMES 1:2-4 MSG

Jesus said, "I've told you all this so that trusting me, you will be
unshakable and assured, deeply at peace. In this godless world you
will continue to experience difficulties. But take heart!
I've conquered the world."
JOHN 16:33 MSG

You, dear children, are from God and have overcome them,
because the one who is in you is greater than the one
who is in the world.
1 JOHN 4:4

Heavenly Father:

I am grateful for Your gift of motherhood, and I realize it was never Your plan for me to do it alone. I have heavenly help that stands ready to assist. So I'm asking for help toward the challenges we face.

Thank You for the angels You've assigned to protect my children and for Your wisdom to guide them safely on their journey through life. I am open and willing to follow Your plan for my life and theirs, and I look to You for the answers we need. You understand each of us individually and I ask You to help us fit together to become the strong family unit You intended.

Regardless of the challenges we face, help me never to magnify my children's shortcomings and failures, but to instead focus on their strengths and successes. I trust You to lead me, as I lead them.

Amen.

THE JERICHO STRATEGY

When Joshua replaced Moses as the military leader in ancient Israel, his very first challenge was the battle of Jericho. Having been nomads for the past forty years and slaves in Egypt prior to that, the Israelites had no experience in warfare. Jericho, on the other hand, was a mighty military fortress surrounded by a great, impenetrable wall. From a human perspective, there was no way the Israelites could win.

As a mom, you have probably already faced a Jericho or two while dealing with parenting issues. You sense that there is a wall that separates you from your child, a fortress erected in defense of his or her emerging identity.

Joshua's experience provides encouragement for the parenting issues you face:

First, Joshua encountered an angel with a sword in his hand. In your situation, heaven's reinforcements are standing ready to assist, if only you'll take the initiative to ask.

Second, the angel told him to take off his sandals while standing in the presence of the Almighty. In Joshua's day, being barefoot signified vulnerability. True faith comes with the willingness to be open and vulnerable to God's strategy for dealing with the challenges you face.

Third, the Lord instructed Joshua to march around the city seven times, blowing trumpets and shouting. Although this battle plan sounded quite odd, Joshua chose to trust God. Even if God's wisdom doesn't line up with your logic, trust Him.

Fourth, the walls of Jericho collapsed as promised. With your children, be ready to move into action when the walls start to fall.

Finally, Joshua rescued a prostitute named Rahab because she had sheltered the Israelite spies from their enemies. He looked past Rahab's occupation to find the good in her. As a mom, you must look past your child's mistakes and reach an understanding of your child's true self.

My Daughter,

I have given you everything you need to guide your children to the destiny I have prepared for them and to help you overcome every challenge. To help you do this, I've given you My Word, which is full of the wisdom you need every single day. Listen for My voice as you read My words, and I will reveal the very thing you need to know.

Just as I continually have you on My mind, I know your children consume many of your thoughts. But do not fear. I have given you the strength and power you need to train them in the way they should go. Together, you and I are preparing them for a wonderful future.

Listen to My instruction in how to love and discipline them, and determine to see them with the same love and concern with which I see you. Encourage them with My Word, just as I encourage you, and I will help all of you to walk the path I've chosen.

Your loving Father

Change

God . . . is looking for those with changed hearts and minds.
Whoever has that kind of change in his life will get
his praise from God.

ROMANS 2:29 TLB

Once you were less than nothing; now you are God's own.
Once you knew very little of God's kindness;
now your very lives have been changed by it.

1 PETER 2:10 TLB

Jesus said, "I tell you the truth, unless you change and become like
little children, you will never enter the kingdom of heaven.
Therefore, whoever humbles himself like this child is
the greatest in the kingdom of heaven."

MATTHEW 18:3-4

Don't become so well-adjusted to your culture that you fit into it
without even thinking. Instead, fix your attention on God. You'll be
changed from the inside out. Readily recognize what he wants from
you, and quickly respond to it. Unlike the culture around you,
always dragging you down to its level of immaturity, God brings the
best out of you, develops well-formed maturity in you.

ROMANS 12:2 MSG

Jesus said, "I gave you an example that you also should do
as I did to you."

JOHN 13:15 NASB

METAMORPHOSIS

"Was he bad again?" The question blurted from her lips as she walked through the doorway.

"Tara, he is never bad," Georgia tried to cut her off before three-year-old Ben heard her. Taking the young woman by the elbow and guiding her into a corner of the room, Georgia continued. "He misbehaves at times, but that doesn't make him bad."

"I don't know why you try to fix my son with your words," she said in frustration. "He was bad, wasn't he?"

"We had another incident today."

"Who'd he bite this time?" Tara turned with a fiery glance, looking for the miniature culprit.

"Tara, I would like to offer another perspective on this situation." Georgia's teaching experience had taught her a great deal about motivating children. "Could you come into my office for a moment?"

Georgia sat across from Ben's mother. "I have noticed something interesting that might give us some insight into how to help Ben handle his anger."

"What?"

"He has the most conflict with other children when the two of you have already had trouble prior to his arrival."

"How do you know when we fight?"

"Trust me, you are like a lit billboard. You prophesy Ben's behavior with amazing accuracy when you drop him off every morning."

"I do?" Her wheels were turning now. "So maybe we would see a change in Ben if I change my attitude toward him?"

"Good thought!" Georgia smiled.

Three weeks later, a bouquet of flowers arrived for Georgia at the preschool. The note said, "Thanks for helping me see that changing my own behavior was the first step toward helping my son change his."

Character

The character of even a child can be known by the
way he acts—whether what he does is pure and right.

PROVERBS 20:11 TLB

Be imitators of God [copy Him and follow His example], as well-
beloved children [imitate their father]. And walk in love, [esteem-
ing and delighting in one another] as Christ loved us and gave
Himself up for us, a slain offering and sacrifice to God.

EPHESIANS 5:1-2 AMP

Dear friend, do not imitate what is evil but what is good.
Anyone who does what is good is from God.

3 JOHN 1:11

One of the teachers of religious law . . . asked [Jesus], "Of all the
commandments, which is the most important?" Jesus replied,
"The most important commandment is this: ' . . . The Lord our
God is the one and only Lord. And you must love the Lord your
God with all your heart, all your soul, all your mind, and all your
strength.' The second is equally important: 'Love your neighbor as
yourself.' No other commandment is greater than these."

MARK 12:28-31 NLT

This is love for God: to obey his commands.
And his commands are not burdensome.

1 JOHN 5:3

A BLUEPRINT FOR NOBLE CHARACTER

Instilling character within a child is the most challenging job a mother faces. How can you convince your child to embrace the values you cherish? To be true to those values throughout his or her life?

Try restating, in language that will motivate and inspire your child, the ten most profound traits of godly character.

- You shall have no other gods before Me. Treat Jesus like your best Friend. He is!
- You shall not make for yourself an idol. God is more awesome than anything you can imagine or desire!
- You shall not misuse the name of the Lord your God. God's name is powerful and worthy of respect—use it accordingly.
- Observe the Sabbath day by keeping it holy. Take time to rest and remember where you came from, where you're going, and whose you are.
- Honor your father and your mother. Treat your family with the respect you think you deserve. Their blood runs through your veins.
- You shall not murder. Value the lives, feelings, and reputations of others. Don't do damage to any of those things.
- You shall not commit adultery. Save your love for the only one worthy of it—your future partner for life.
- You shall not steal. Respect and protect the property of others.
- You shall not give false testimony. Be known as a person of integrity.
- You shall not covet anything that belongs to others. Be content with who you are and with what you have.

If you will become creative and courageous about how to demonstrate and reinforce these ideals, your child will likely become a person of noble character.

Commitment

[The Lord] always stands by his covenant—
the commitment he made to a thousand generations.

1 CHRONICLES 16:15 NLT

Depend on it: God keeps his word even when the whole world
is lying through its teeth. Scripture says the same:
Your words stand fast and true.

ROMANS 3:4 MSG

Make sure that you don't get so absorbed and exhausted
in taking care of all your day-by-day obligations that you lose track
of the time and doze off, oblivious to God.

ROMANS 13:11 MSG

What happens when we live God's way?
. . . We develop a willingness to stick with things. . . .
We find ourselves involved in loyal commitments.

GALATIANS 5:22 MSG

We'll stick to our assigned tasks of prayer and speaking God's Word.

ACTS 6:4 MSG

Each person must be responsible for himself.

GALATIANS 6:5 NCV

Heavenly Father:

Keeping commitments is important to You, and I realize it is my responsibility to instill this value into my children. I also realize that it must first begin with me.

Sometimes circumstances and schedules make it difficult for me to keep my commitments. I'm tempted to justify my actions because it's easier to say, "I don't have a choice"—but in my heart, I know I do. Often I overcommit because I don't want to disappoint others, yet this sets me up to fail because I can't possibly do all I've said I would.

Father, You know where I need to spend my time and which relationships I need to give energy to. Show me which commitments I should make and how to graciously say no when I might commit to too many things at once. I don't ever want to be known as a promise-breaker. Help me to be an example that my children will be proud to follow. Thank You, Father.

Amen.

A PROMISE TO MY HEART

One of God's friends in the Bible expressed a novel approach to keeping commitments. Job said, "I made a covenant with my eyes not to look lustfully at a girl" (Job 31:1). He honored his commitment to marriage by treating his eyes as though they were partners.

As a mom, you can provide invaluable assistance by modeling your commitments in various aspects of your life in similar ways. When watching television, for instance, you may say, "I'm going to turn the channel because I've made a promise to my eyes that I won't make them watch acts of violence." Or when selecting a book, "I made a commitment to my heart that I won't read anything that will cause me to be afraid." An example related to diet and nutrition: "I promised my bones that I will take good care of them, so I think I'll have milk instead of cola."

When it comes to relationships, commitments are two-sided, running in both directions—to oneself and to the one with whom you are related. You might find it helpful to suggest something such as: "I made a promise to my heart that I will never say anything about Candice that would wound her."

Keeping commitments is difficult work for youngsters. Helping them see their bodies and minds as partners in promise-keeping is one way to help motivate them for greater success.

My Daughter,

You're right—commitment is very important to Me. As you know, I always keep My Word, and I never break My promises. And I treasure those who do the same. They bless Me and are a great blessing to those whose lives they touch.

A godly woman is one of commitment. Her word is her bond, and her reputation precedes her and brings her honor. As you live your life before your children, placing a high value on always following through on what you've committed to do, you set a higher standard that they will be encouraged to follow.

Jesus led by example during His earthly ministry, saying, "I do nothing on my own but speak just what the Father has taught me" (John 8:28). As you consistently do as He did, your children will do as you do.

Your loving Father

Communication

Speaking the truth in love, we are to grow up in all aspects
into Him who is the head, even Christ.

EPHESIANS 4:15 NASB

Let your speech always be with grace, as though seasoned with salt,
so that you will know how you should respond to each person.

COLOSSIANS 4:6 NASB

Always be willing to listen and slow to speak.
Do not become angry easily, because anger will not help you
live the right kind of life God wants.

JAMES 1:19-20 NCV

A soft answer turns away wrath,
but a harsh word stirs up anger.

PROVERBS 15:1 NRSV

Gentle words cause life and health;
griping brings discouragement.

PROVERBS 15:4 TLB

Wise people's minds tell them what to say.

PROVERBS 16:23 NCV

CARING ENOUGH TO LISTEN

"Face it, Mom, you really don't care what I think," Mandy shouted, slamming the door as she left. Backing recklessly out of the driveway, the tires squealed as she sped away.

Sue stood looking out the window listening to her daughter's words echo through her mind. As much as she hated to admit it, she really didn't care what Mandy thought. It seemed that she and Mandy didn't see anything alike. If Sue wanted her to wear a dress for special occasions, Mandy was sure to appear in tight, hip-hugger shorts. If Sue announced a family dinner plan, Mandy made arrangements to be with friends.

This morning had been no different. Sue had awakened Mandy with annoying cheerfulness. "Time to get up, Kiddo—it's a beautiful day, and you're missing it!" She knew she was going over the top. She did this most mornings, on purpose, because it irked her that her daughter overslept every day.

Mandy groaned and pulled the blanket over her head. Sue snatched the blanket away, the fake cheerfulness evaporating. "Not a chance. Up. You have responsibilities, too, you know."

"Does it ever occur to you why I might sleep late?" Mandy asked, frustrated. She rolled over and mumbled through her pillow, "I was up until four studying for my biology exam."

"And I've been up since 5:30 getting ready for work and making you breakfast," Sue responded, unsympathetically.

"But I don't want breakfast," Mandy protested. "I never want breakfast. I tell you this every day. Why can't you listen to me for once?"

But Sue just left the room.

Now, Sue moved from the window to her desk. Pulling out pen and paper, she wrote: Dear Mandy, you were right. I haven't really cared what you think, but I wasn't aware of it until you pointed it out. I realize how that must make you feel. Will you forgive me? Love, Mom.

Compassion

Praise be to the God and Father of our Lord Jesus Christ, the Father of compassion and the God of all comfort, who comforts us in all our troubles, so that we can comfort those in any trouble with the comfort we ourselves have received from God.

2 CORINTHIANS 1:3-4

When Jesus went out He saw a great multitude;
and He was moved with compassion for them.

MATTHEW 14:14 NKJV

God is fair; he will not forget the work you did and
the love you showed for him by helping his people.
And he will remember that you are still helping them.

HEBREWS 6:10 NCV

The Lord is good to everyone.
He showers compassion on all his creation.

PSALM 145:9 NLT

Light arises in the darkness for the upright;
He is gracious and compassionate and righteous.

PSALM 112:4 NASB

A MOTHER KNOWS

People were packed in chairs at every gate, frustration glaring from every face. Marcie slumped into the last remaining seat, tears raining onto her linen skirt and staining it with salty deposits.

Marcie despised traveling, especially since the birth of her son, Bryan. She had thought that it wouldn't be too difficult— leaving town twice a month for an overnight stay, two nights at most. But that was before the baby had been diagnosed with a rare blood disease. Now Bryan was on his way to the hospital for a blood transfusion, and she was stuck in an airport in Memphis.

"Excuse me," a voice spoke from above her.

Glancing up, Marcie was shocked to find a white-haired woman standing directly over her. "Oh, I'm sorry," she apologized, gathering her things.

"No, you're fine," she said reassuringly. "I happened to be standing at the counter when you explained your son's emergency situation."

Marcie blinked.

"I have a seat on the only flight leaving Memphis headed for Dallas tonight. Would you allow me to trade flights with you?"

"But who knows how long you could be stuck here?" Marcie argued, standing up to face her.

"Long or short, you cannot afford to wait, my dear," she smiled. "Let's get you home to the little guy."

At that, the floodgates burst. Marcie fell into the woman's arms and wept with relief. "How can I ever thank you?"

"No need. I'm a mother too." She smiled, brushing a stream of tears from Marcie's face with her thumb.

There is a compassion borne of empathy that only mothers share.

Confidence

The Fear-of-God builds up confidence,
and makes a world safe for your children.
PROVERBS 14:26 MSG

The steps of the godly are directed by the Lord. . . .
Though they stumble, they will not fall,
for the Lord holds them by the hand.
PSALM 37:23-24 NLT

O Lord God, You are my confidence.
PSALM 71:5 NASB

The Lord will be your confidence
and will keep your foot from being snared.
PROVERBS 3:26

The fruit of righteousness will be peace;
the effect of righteousness will be quietness and confidence forever.
My people will live in peaceful dwelling places,
in secure homes, in undisturbed places of rest.
ISAIAH 32:17-18

Heavenly Father:

Sometimes I'm tempted to compare myself with other mothers—especially those who seem to be doing everything right—and I always seem to come up short. Only You know how hard I try and how much it means to me to be a successful mother.

More than anything, I want my children to become all You want them to be, but sometimes I am overwhelmed by such a huge responsibility. When I make mistakes or things go wrong, I second-guess myself, worry, and wonder if I'm doing enough.

But then I come back to You and realize that You chose me to raise my precious children. With Your vote of confidence, I can stand strong knowing that I won't fail as long as I allow You to show me the right steps toward being the mother that my children truly need.

Amen.

A GOOD MOMMY FOR JACOB

"If you want your confidence knocked out from under you, just go to the park and have a chat with the local confederation of lactating zealots!" Ginny shouted as she flung her purse onto the couch.

"Honey, what happened?" Mitchell asked, unzipping the jacket of their three-year-old son, Jacob.

"When that militant band of nursing mothers gangs up . . . well, let's just say the whole thing hit the fan today."

"What whole thing?" Mitchell's brow knitted with concern.

"The ever-so-perfect Alyson just laid into me about the never-so-robust immune system of our son," Ginny's face was splotched red. "She implied that had I nursed Jacob, he would be a healthier child."

"Honey, are you sure that's what she said?" Mitch moved closer to console her.

"No," she murmured as she sniffed back tears.

"No what?"

"That's not exactly what she said."

"Well, what then?" he pressed.

"She said that formula manufacturers have worked hard to reproduce the effects of a mother's milk on an infant's immune system, but they haven't yet been able to," Ginny cried.

"And that upset you?" Mitchell struggled to understand.

"I want to be a good mommy for Jacob," she wailed, "but I can't seem to get it all right!"

Jacob sidled up to his mother and hugged her thigh really tight. "Good Mommy for Jacob," he consoled.

Sometimes the opinions of others can undermine the confidence of a very good mother. No mom will ever be perfect, no matter how hard she tries, but with God's help, you can be "just right" for the children He's given you.

My Daughter,

Children don't arrive with an owner's manual and I know that can seem scary, especially in this crazy, mixed-up world. When you feel insecure, it might seem easiest to follow the latest parenting trends, but many of them contradict each other and none come with a guarantee.

What you must realize is that there are no cookie-cutter children. I have created each one to be unique, and I've given yours to you to shape and mold according to My plan for their lives.

Rest assured, I've provided everything you need to parent them effectively. First and foremost, I've given you My Word, which is full of all the wisdom you'll ever need. And you also have the Holy Spirit, your own personal tutor. Look to Me for the answers you need, and I will direct your steps. Never forget, you have My vote of confidence!

Your loving Father

Conflict

Stay away from foolish and stupid arguments, because you know
they grow into quarrels. And a servant of the Lord must not quarrel
but must be kind to everyone, a good teacher, and patient.
The Lord's servant must gently teach those who disagree.
Then maybe God will let them change their minds
so they can accept the truth.

2 TIMOTHY 2:23-25 NCV

Work at getting along with each other and with God.
Otherwise you'll never get so much as a glimpse of God.

HEBREWS 12:14 MSG

Pride only breeds quarrels,
but wisdom is found in those who take advice.

PROVERBS 13:10

Those who control their anger have great understanding;
those with a hasty temper will make mistakes.

PROVERBS 14:29 NLT

People with good sense restrain their anger.

PROVERBS 19:11 NLT

FIGHT RIGHT!

Unfortunately, conflict is an inevitable part of life, and raising children provides ample opportunities to experience it firsthand. There is good news, however. Experts tell us there are some key principles that can help you keep your perspective on the value of the relationship while engaged in the heat of battle.

- Remember that conflict is a normal part of being in a relationship. If there is never any conflict, there is probably a deficiency in the relationship. When you sense that tension is building between you and one of your children, learn to view it as an opportunity to grow even closer.
- Conflict provides a tremendous opportunity for understanding. Assess the reason for the conflict, and take pause to determine the validity of your child's perspective. Children can teach you amazing things—if you are open to them.
- Recognize that because conflict is the result of diversity, it provides an invaluable opportunity to demonstrate respect for your children. This requires that you allow them to express their feelings and opinions freely while you listen objectively without feeling the need to make a judgment or fix their perspective.
- The most critical objectives in conflict are resolution, mutual understanding, and a deeper connection within the heart. It is important to remember that being right is not the objective. The only true victory is that in which both parties share.
- Finally, having given full vent to both sides of an issue, and having resolved a reasonable solution, clear the air with some genuine joy and hearty laughter. Maintain a healthy sense of humor. The ability to "get past it" and "move on" is a mark of true maturity.

Contentment

Keep your lives free from the love of money
and be content with what you have,
because God has said, "Never will I leave you;
never will I forsake you."

HEBREWS 13:5

Better a little with righteousness
than much gain with injustice.

PROVERBS 16:8

I have learned how to get along happily whether I have much or
little. I know how to live on almost nothing or with everything.
I have learned the secret of contentment in every situation.

PHILIPPIANS 4:11-12 TLB

Godliness with contentment is great gain. . . .
If we have food and clothing, we will be content with that.

1 TIMOTHY 6:6,8

The fear of the Lord leads to life:
Then one rests content, untouched by trouble.

PROVERBS 19:23

THE SECRET OF CONTENTMENT

"If we could just buy a bigger house, I'd be happy." "I wish your father would get a better-paying job." "I wish I had some time to myself." "Why can't you be like Joey and bring home a decent report card?" "If I could just lose some weight, had better hair, were prettier . . ."

You may be unaware of how many ways throughout the day you express your lack of contentment to your child. The apostle Paul wrote: "I have learned the secret of being content in any and every situation" (Philippians 4:12).

The secret of contentment lies not in focusing upon what you lack, but in concentrating deeply upon those things of value with which you have been entrusted. For instance, when you learn to value the people in your life appropriately, material things diminish in importance and you find contentment in your relationships. When you learn to cherish truth and spiritual growth, temporal things pale in comparison and you experience great joy. When you learn to value integrity, nurture humility, love unconditionally, and become more invested in the happiness of others than in yourself, the pettiness of dissatisfaction melts away and the result is abundant life.

Contentment is contagious. It is one of those elusive traits that children learn more effectively by example than any other way. So the question is, have you learned the secret of being content? If not, you can begin changing that today. The result will be a happier you and children more at peace.

Courage

Be strong in the Lord and in the power of His might.
Put on the whole armor of God, that you may be able to stand
against the wiles of the devil.

EPHESIANS 6:10-11 NKJV

Keep alert, stand firm in your faith, be courageous, be strong.

1 CORINTHIANS 16:13 NRSV

Don't lose your courage or be afraid. Don't panic or be frightened,
because the Lord your God goes with you, to fight for you against
your enemies and to save you.

DEUTERONOMY 20:3-4 NCV

Lord, you are my shield,
my wonderful God who gives me courage.

PSALM 3:3 NCV

Do not lose the courage you had in the past,
which has a great reward. You must hold on, so you can do
what God wants and receive what he has promised.

HEBREWS 10:35-36 NCV

Be strong and courageous. Do not be afraid or terrified
because of them, for the Lord your God goes with you;
he will never leave you nor forsake you.

DEUTERONOMY 31:6

Heavenly Father:

I want to be wise in inspiring my children. I want to help them be bold and courageous, endeavoring to live out their dreams. At the same time, though, I hesitate because I don't want to see their hearts disappointed.

There are so many times in life that I've faced disappointment and struggled to find the courage to take the next step. I don't want my children to experience that; I want them to enjoy their childhood. It's hard for me to watch them—so full of hope and expectation—and sometimes see them fall into disappointment.

I want—and I know You want—them to succeed at every challenge in life and maintain the courage to remain willing to try again and again to achieve that goal. Help me to build them up and give them the courage to succeed.

Amen.

GOD WILL FIGHT FOR YOU

"What are you doing here?" Eliab, David's oldest brother, scolded.

"I've brought food," David answered.

"I suspect you're really here to satiate a morbid curiosity," Eliab challenged his youngest brother.

"No," David argued, "but how can God's army allow that man to talk to them like that?"

Goliath, a warrior—standing nearly ten feet tall—had for forty days challenged the Israelites to send a man to face him in battle. If the Israelites won, the enemy would become their servants. If the enemy won, Israel would be enslaved. There wasn't a single man willing to risk his life so foolishly.

"How brave of you to criticize us," Eliab chided sarcastically. "Even if one of us were to give his life for this cause, Israel would still be the loser. What can I do?"

"It's not about you," replied David. "The battle belongs to the Lord."

"Sure," Eliab mocked. "This is God's army, right? Well, why hasn't He shown up to fight the giant?"

"He has," David assured him. "Every time a lion or a bear attacks my sheep, the Lord helps me defeat them. He will do the same thing here. With God, all things are possible," David continued. "I'll meet this giant on his terms."

"You can't win," Eliab countered. "You're taking this God thing too far."

Yet Goliath fell to the courage of a shepherd boy with a slingshot and true faith. (See 1 Samuel 17.)

When it comes to courage, a child's greatest advantage is his or her idealism. Soon enough, they learn that the good guys don't always win. But be careful not to snuff out that tender wick with an untimely dose of realism.

My Daughter,

Childhood is a time for children to fly high with their imaginations. It's filled with a strong dose of optimism and thoughts such as: *If I think I can, I can.* They often perceive themselves as invincible, able to do and be anything their hearts dare to dream.

But there will be times of disappointment, when the circumstances of life will zap their strength and bring them down. It's as if they are traveling the world in a helium balloon. Yet over time, helium will escape, their faith may dwindle, and they will come down to earth, to reality.

As a mother, it's your responsibility to fuel your children's passion and instill the courage they need to try and try again. Give them My Word and help them discover My will for their lives. Teach them how to put their faith in Me and how to stand strong and courageous. There will be times of disappointment, but if they won't give up, I will help them get through those times and give them a life beyond their wildest dreams.

Your loving Father

Decisions

I will instruct you and teach you in the way you should go;
I will counsel you and watch over you.

PSALM 32:8

Jesus said, "Father . . . not My will, but Yours, be done."

LUKE 22:42 NKJV

I am the Lord your God,
who teaches you what is best for you,
who directs you in the way you should go.

ISAIAH 48:17

Let each of you look out not only for his own interests,
but also for the interests of others.

PHILIPPIANS 2:4 NKJV

Think of yourselves the way Christ Jesus thought of himself.
He had equal status with God but didn't think so much of himself
that he had to cling to the advantages of that status no matter what.
Not at all. When the time came, he set aside the privileges of deity
and took on the status of a slave, became human! . . . He lived a
selfless, obedient life and then died a selfless, obedient death.

PHILIPPIANS 2:5-8 MSG

THE DECISION TO BE UNSELFISH

Moms begin teaching children decision-making skills as soon as they are able to communicate—giving them options from which they may choose.

"Do you want cereal or waffles for breakfast?"

Soon the child takes the initiative in making decisions by expressing their preferences and desires.

Allowing your child to make simple decisions gives them a sense of empowerment and a healthy awareness of their individuality. Throughout their lives, they hone and develop those skills in order to become responsible adults who function well in society.

There comes a time in children's lives, however, when decision-making needs to be tempered with unselfishness, when serving the needs and desires of others must come before fulfilling their own.

"Mom, Sara asked me to go to a movie, but Missy needs help with her science project. What should I do?"

This kind of decision-making gives children the opportunity to reflect the nature of God, the character you most want your child to emulate. God's decision to share His nature and His nobility, as well as to delegate some of His authority to man on earth, was an unselfish and risky decision. During His earthly life, Jesus made the unselfish decision to serve instead of being served.

Teaching children these principles is certainly important, but the fact remains that children will effectively learn only what they see modeled at home. That means that your decision-making processes must track down the same path. Are you up to the challenge?

Discretion

Wisdom will enter your heart,
and knowledge will be pleasant to your soul.
Discretion will protect you,
and understanding will guard you.

PROVERBS 2:10-11

Pay attention to my wisdom,
listen well to my words of insight,
that you may maintain discretion
and your lips may preserve knowledge.

PROVERBS 5:1-2

Keep sound wisdom and discretion,
So they will be life to your soul.

PROVERBS 3:21-22 NASB

Discretion is a life-giving fountain to those who possess it,
but discipline is wasted on fools.

PROVERBS 16:22 NLT

SOME THINGS ARE BEST UNSAID

"Hezekiah, who are those men leaving the city just now?" the aged prophet Isaiah asked. Isaiah had been the spiritual counselor to the king of Judah ever since King Hezekiah's great-grandfather had been in power. Skeptical of the sovereign's discernment, he felt the need to inquire.

"They came from Babylon with a get-well gift," Hezekiah replied as he held proudly to the edges of his regal attire, convinced of his prominence among foreign dignitaries. The visiting embassy had stroked his craving for the esteem of men of status.

"What did they say?" Isaiah probed further. The sage was disturbed, having observed the strangers studying the structure of Jerusalem's protective walls.

"They said that the king of Babylon was greatly alarmed to hear of my recent brush with death."

"So you discussed your recent illness?" The prophet tamed his beard with the palm of his hand. "What other information did you share with them?"

"Everything!" Hezekiah boasted. "Considering how affected they were that the Lord's favor was upon me, I showed them my wealth, military strength, and political strategy. They were quite impressed!"

"Hezekiah, do you realize that your poor judgment has put us all in jeopardy? This indiscretion will come back to haunt you." And sadly, it did. (See 2 Kings 20 and Isaiah 39.)

As a mother, you probably already know that children have a tendency to be too trusting. They can be easily taken in, especially by flattering words. While you don't want to instill fear, it is wise to teach your children to be cautious, prudent, and discreet. Your example, of course, is the best teacher. As situations arise, verbalize why discretion is needed and how to put it into practice.

Encouragement

Encourage one another daily, as long as it is called Today,
so that none of you may be hardened by sin's deceitfulness.

HEBREWS 3:13

Let us therefore make every effort to do what leads to peace
and to mutual edification.

ROMANS 14:19

Encourage each other. Live in harmony and peace.

2 CORINTHIANS 13:11 NLT

With each of you we were like a father with his child, holding your
hand, whispering encouragement, showing you step-by-step how to
live well before God, who called us into his own kingdom,
into this delightful life.

1 THESSALONIANS 2:11-12 MSG

Do not let any unwholesome talk come out of your mouths, but
only what is helpful for building others up according to their needs,
that it may benefit those who listen.

EPHESIANS 4:29

Anxious hearts are very heavy but
a word of encouragement does wonders!

PROVERBS 12:25 TLB

Heavenly Father:

I want to encourage my children and others around me. I don't mean to dwell on negative traits, but so often that is what I notice first. Help me to notice the positive qualities in others instead.

I know it's my job to train my children, to discipline and correct them when they miss the mark, but too often my words have a negative tone that discourages them. It hurts me when I see the hurt on their faces. Help me to find words that are empowering and encouraging.

Lord, just as Your Word often comforts me and provides me with the affirmation I need to grow in excellence of character, word, and action, cause my words to do the same for the children You've given to me. Help me to influence them for good so that they can become all You desire them to be.

Amen.

HONEY TO THE SOUL

Do you remember how it felt when you were in elementary school and had difficulty grasping a concept in math? Or, perhaps the science theorems all seemed to run together? One little girl cried herself to sleep at night after her first-grade teacher had introduced the concept of telling time: "I'll never get it, Mama. It's just too hard." For a child, life can be overwhelming.

Continuing down that path of memories, do you recall how a positive word of encouragement could turn everything around, shifting your perspective from hopelessness to a sensation near giddiness? The power of a positive word is a radical force for good within the heart of a child, carrying with it the seed of potential and increasing the child's chance for success. Likewise, withholding those much-needed expressions of reassurance can cause something within the child to wither and die.

Genuine encouragement is comprised of some elements worthy of your consideration. First, in order to be effective, words of encouragement must be true. Even children can discern between what is genuine and what is insincere.

Next, it should be challenging, leading to the development of a more noble character. Effective affirmation will reinforce admirable traits within the child, which promote excellence in character.

Finally, your words of encouragement should target those things truly worthy of praise, reinforcing behaviors which will lead the child to develop into a godly person of deep integrity.

Everyone needs to hear words of encouragement for they are like honey to the soul. Say them sincerely and say them often.

My Daughter,

One of the most beautiful sounds your children hear is your voice singing their praises. Encouragement builds them up and strengthens them so they can continue successfully toward the destiny I've planned for them. Like sunshine, rain, and good soil enable a flower to blossom and thrive, your words of encouragement feed the hungry souls of your children.

Yes, negative behavior must be dealt with, but follow My example. Condemnation never comes from Me but from My adversary who seeks to destroy. When I discipline those I love, I always do it in a way that encourages My children to come up to a higher level. I correct, but I also extend forgiveness and restoration.

I have given you the ability to have a tremendous influence over your children. Use this power wisely, always for good, to encourage them toward a lifestyle that will bless them and glorify Me.

Your loving Father

Expectations

A word to you parents. Don't keep on scolding and nagging your children, making them angry and resentful. Rather, bring them up with the loving discipline the Lord himself approves, with suggestions and godly advice.

EPHESIANS 6:4 TLB

Parents, don't come down too hard on your children or you'll crush their spirits.

COLOSSIANS 3:21 MSG

Real wisdom, God's wisdom, begins with a holy life and is characterized by getting along with others. It is gentle and reasonable, overflowing with mercy and blessings.

JAMES 3:17 MSG

When she speaks, her words are wise, and kindness is the rule when she gives instructions. . . . Her children stand and bless her.

PROVERBS 31:26,28 NLT

Happiness comes to those who are fair to others and are always just and good.

PSALM 106:3 TLB

The Lord loves justice and fairness.

PSALM 37:28 TLB

TOO MUCH FOR ONE

"I am so disappointed in you!" Tom's mother slammed her books onto the counter.

"What did you expect me to do?" his defenses flew up.

"I expected you to mow the yard like you were told!" she yelled. "I can't do everything around here and finish my degree too."

"Has it ever occurred to you that maybe you expect too much? It's nearly a hundred degrees out there!" he snapped. Ever since the divorce, there was so much pressure on him. Reluctantly he made his way to the garage and started the mower. The task was sure to prove grueling.

Inside, Melinda slumped into an overstuffed chair and watched her son from the window. She swiped a tear from her cheek at the same moment he wiped the first stream of sweat from his forehead. "Poor guy," she said out loud. "It isn't his fault that his dad and I couldn't work things out."

Twenty scorching minutes crawled by when suddenly Tom caught a glimpse of his mom carrying a tray of lemonade and cookies out to him.

"What's this?" he asked as he put the mower on idle.

"Thought you could use a break," she said, smiling. After handing him the tray, she grabbed the handle of the mower and pushed on.

After ten minutes, Tom met his mother coming around the far side of the house. "My turn!" he announced.

High standards are important, but expecting too much is counterproductive and even destructive. And it can cause you to think less of your children than you should. Ask for God's wisdom to know if you cross the line, and be sure to applaud when your reasonable expectations are met.

Faith

I am mindful of the sincere faith within you,
which first dwelt in your grandmother Lois and your mother
Eunice, and I am sure that it is in you as well.

2 TIMOTHY 1:5 NASB

Cling tightly to your faith in Christ and always keep your conscience
clear, doing what you know is right.

1 TIMOTHY 1:19 TLB

Be their ideal; let them follow the way you teach and live; be a
pattern for them in your love, your faith, and your clean thoughts.

1 TIMOTHY 4:12 TLB

Look closely at yourselves.
Test yourselves to see if you are living in the faith.

2 CORINTHIANS 13:5 NCV

As you received Christ Jesus the Lord, so continue to live in him.
Keep your roots deep in him and have your lives built on him.
Be strong in the faith.

COLOSSIANS 2:6-7 NCV

Hold on to the pattern of right teaching you learned. . . . And
remember to live in the faith and love that you have in Christ Jesus.

2 TIMOTHY 1:13 NLT

FAITH YOU CAN SEE

"Hannah," he approached her gingerly, as if his voice might cause her to shatter. "It's time to go."

"I know," she wiped the wetness from her face with her shawl. "I'll go get him. I just didn't want him to see me crying."

"You don't have to do this, you know," he said, putting his hand on her shoulder.

"But I made a promise . . ." she ducked out from under Elkanah's touch, trying to dodge her own emotions, and headed out the door to collect her small son for the long trip to Shiloh.

Little Samuel was too young to understand. The depth of his mother's pain in parting concerned and confused him, especially since the old priest with whom she was leaving him was a total stranger. Eli, she called him.

Samuel lay awake many nights on his little cot longing for home, missing the tenderness of his mother's love. He never doubted her, though she had left him. He kept her words in his heart: "You were a gift from the Lord, and I promised I would give you back to Him."

One night, the Lord called him by name. At first, Samuel thought it was Eli.

"Answer Him," Eli counseled, "for this is the One to whom your mother dedicated you."

Samuel grew up to become the spiritual leader of the nation of Israel. His faith afforded him a powerful and intimate relationship with the Lord, all because his mother, Hannah, was true to her own faith. You can read their story in I Samuel 1-3.

Faithfulness

Oh, love the Lord, all you His saints!
For the Lord preserves the faithful.

PSALM 31:23 NKJV

The fruit of the Spirit is . . . faithfulness.

GALATIANS 5:22 NASB

How thankful I am to Christ Jesus our Lord for . . .
giving me the strength to be faithful to him.

1 TIMOTHY 1:12 TLB

If we are faithful to the end, trusting God
just as we did when we first became Christians,
we will share in all that belongs to Christ.

HEBREWS 3:14 TLB

O Jehovah, Commander of the heavenly armies,
where is there any other Mighty One like you?
Faithfulness is your very character.

PSALM 89:8 TLB

Women . . . must be serious, not slanderers,
but temperate, faithful in all things.

1 TIMOTHY 3:11 NRSV

Heavenly Father:

You have given me a priceless treasure in my children, and I want to be found faithful in my responsibility to raise them according to Your design. I want to do everything I can to help them become all that You created them to be.

Help me to recognize it if I ever try to mold them into my own likeness or push them to embrace my own childhood dreams. Instead, use me to instill in them a great desire to fulfill their God-given destiny.

Allow me to discover the things within them that fuel their passion and show me how to bring their gifts forward in Your timing. Give me the words to validate their actions as they step out toward the life You've prepared for them. And when it comes time—help me to let them go.

Amen.

DELIGHT IN GOD'S DESIGN

Some people think that keeping a checklist is the only way to prove one's faithfulness. The problem with checklists is that they address merely what lies on the surface of life—behavior, actions, rituals, etc.—but they are ineffective at penetrating the hearts of people, and especially your children.

For example, you can post a checklist for your child on the refrigerator: brush your teeth, clean your room, take out the trash, feed the dog, complete your homework. But notice, no checklist includes things such as having a heart-to-heart talk about the boy who wrote the love note in science class yesterday; apologizing to the brother to whom insulting remarks were made; praying as a family about the latest terrorist attack; or writing a dark poem late in the night after a friend at school attempted suicide.

Another common error concerning faithfulness lies behind the idea that parents are to recreate children into their own image, or worse, push them to become what they failed to become: doctors, lawyers, or supermodels. As a mom, it is your job to validate God's creation by discovering who your children were designed to be and delighting in their freedom to fulfill their purpose in life.

Real relationship penetrates beneath the surface issues of life and reaches into the depths of your children's hearts, touching the essence of their beings. Faithfulness is the relentless pursuit of discovering the truth about your children, combined with the radical acceptance and appreciation that affirms God's design.

My Daughter,

Sometimes My standard for godly parents can seem unattainable, overwhelming, but it's not. It's about being faithful in the little things—the way you respond to your children when they please you and when they don't. It's about correcting them in love and praising them for choosing right over wrong.

My servant Abraham was faithful in the little things. When I told him to leave his people, he trusted Me and faithfully journeyed in the direction I gave him, one day at a time. Eventually his faithfulness paid off and he fulfilled My plan for his life—becoming the father of many nations.

Lean on the Holy Spirit, your teacher, to show you how to faithfully and consistently influence your children for Me. Then watch as little by little they blossom into the incredible people I've designed them to be.

Your loving Father

Family

The Lord God said, "It is not good that man should be alone;
I will make him a helper comparable to him."
GENESIS 2:18 NKJV

Male and female He created them. Then God blessed them,
and God said to them, "Be fruitful and multiply;
fill the earth and subdue it."
GENESIS 1:27-28 NKJV

You should be like one big happy family, full of sympathy
toward each other, loving one another with tender hearts
and humble minds.
1 PETER 3:8 TLB

How wonderful, how beautiful,
when brothers and sisters get along! . . .
That's where God commands the blessing,
ordains eternal life.
PSALM 133:1,3 MSG

Try always to be led along together by the Holy Spirit,
and so be at peace with one another.
EPHESIANS 4:3 TLB

FACE-TO-FACE, DAY-BY-DAY

The Bible doesn't contain a formula for the perfect family. It doesn't say that every Thursday night should be family night or that you should homeschool your children. The Word of God doesn't say that family vacations are important or even that you should have family devotions.

What the Bible does say a great deal about is our responsibilities in relationship to "one another."

· Love one another.
· Pray for one another.
· Sing to one another.
· Confess to one another.

According to the Scriptures, the philosophy which will produce a family that honors God and others holds forth a simple premise that Jesus himself modeled: "Do nothing out of selfish ambition or vain conceit, but in humility consider others better than yourselves. Each of you should look not only to your own interests, but also to the interests of others" (Philippians 2:3-4).

Sounds like a pretty solid foundation for family, doesn't it?

Keep in mind, the family isn't an institution that you are trying to preserve and promote. Parents must teach children to be committed to one another, one individual at a time. Each person is personally responsible for the well-being of every other person within the family. If one child is struggling, he or she needs the love, care, and support of each sibling and parent—one by one.

Don't take for granted that having the same last name, eating at the same table, and sharing the same house means that love is present. There simply are no shortcuts to becoming the kind of family that is truly committed. It must be cultivated and nurtured face-to-face, day-by-day.

Fear

I call to you from the ends of the earth
when I am afraid.
Carry me away to a high mountain.
You have been my protection,
like a strong tower against my enemies.

PSALM 61:2-3 NCV

I am the Lord, your God,
who takes hold of your right hand
and says to you, Do not fear;
I will help you.

ISAIAH 41:13

Don't be afraid, for I am with you. Do not be dismayed,
for I am your God. I will strengthen you. I will help you.
I will uphold you with my victorious right hand.

ISAIAH 41:10 NLT

When I am afraid, I will put my confidence in you.
Yes, I will trust the promises of God.

PSALM 56:3-4 TLB

God has not given us a spirit of fear,
but of power and of love and of a sound mind.

2 TIMOTHY 1:7 NKJV

RESCUING THE FUTURE

"But, Lord, I am not qualified to do the job."

"I will be with you," the Lord consoled him.

"But I don't have an impressive heritage, nor have I ever accomplished anything worthy of mention," Gideon argued.

"Just trust Me, Gideon. That's all I need from you."

The cruel enemy had oppressed Israel for seven years, driving God's people into exile, forcing them to hide in caves like animals. Mere survival consumed their desperate days, and fear of terrors plagued them at night. Had Israel simply been faithful to God, none of this would have happened. But they weren't, and it did. So God appeared to a young man with an honest heart and commissioned him to deliver the entire nation.

"Where do I begin?" Gideon inquired.

"By confronting your own family," the Lord insisted. "Start by putting a stop to the destructive behaviors from your past."

Gideon feared no one as much as he feared his family and friends. The youngest of his tribe, he had no influence or authority. *They will never listen to me*, he reasoned.

In spite of his fear, Gideon mustered the courage to break down his father's pagan altars under the cloak of darkness, while no one was looking.

Just as he suspected, everyone was furious with him. "Hand him over," they demanded of Gideon's father. "He must die."

Surprisingly, Gideon's father defended him. And as a result of confronting the ungodly behavior within his own family, he then had the courage to face the enemy. (See Judges 6:1-32.)

The fear of addressing shortcomings and failures of the past can be overwhelming. But once confronted and addressed, you will find the courage to rescue your children's future.

Forgiveness

Bear with each other and forgive whatever grievances you may have
against one another. Forgive as the Lord forgave you.

COLOSSIANS 3:13

Peter came to Jesus and asked, "Lord, how many times shall I
forgive my brother when he sins against me? Up to seven times?"
Jesus answered, "I tell you, not seven times,
but seventy-seven times."

MATTHEW 18:21-22

If you forgive anyone, I also forgive him.
And what I have forgiven—if there was anything to forgive—
I have forgiven in the sight of Christ for your sake.

2 CORINTHIANS 2:10

You will again have compassion on us;
you will tread our sins underfoot and hurl
all our iniquities into the depths of the sea.

MICAH 7:19

Jesus said, "Whenever you stand praying, forgive,
if you have anything against anyone, so that your Father who is
in heaven will also forgive you your transgressions."

MARK 11:25 NASB

Heavenly Father:

I want to leave the past behind; I want to forgive and forget, but sometimes forgetting seems impossible. No one can hurt me like my husband or children, and when they do, I find myself wanting to make them pay for it. It is especially difficult to forgive when the same offenses are committed over and over again.

I want to let go and truly forgive. Help me to tear down the walls of the past and remove the negative memories that want to hold me in bitterness. Help me to focus on the positive aspects of our relationship and do my part to make our home a loving one.

I don't want us to simply sweep problems under the rug, because that will only result in more problems. Instead, help us to resolve our conflicts, to forgive each other and ourselves, and then to move on. Help us to forgive as You do.

Amen.

BREAKING TRUST

The wealthy old man rises from the evening meal and walks to the crest of the hill outside his dwelling. Squinting into the blaze of the setting sun, he shields his eyes and searches the landscape with an intense gaze. Every day he comes, ever since his son left home.

Tears sting his eyes as he stands looking. With winter coming on, he worries about the boy's whereabouts. He recalls the tender years of the boy's youth—the laughter and the love, the warmth of his embrace. But in recent years, the young man had thrust a dagger of disrespect into his old heart and twisted it with betrayal. He had taken his inheritance and abandoned his father.

One of the young stewards approaches and stands beside the old man.

"Why don't you quit torturing yourself like this, Sir? He isn't coming back."

The patriarch lingers in the silence for several minutes. Finally, he speaks, "I'll never give up."

It is in that moment that a silhouette appears in the distance against the sky. Suddenly, the great heart of the man seizes with recognition. It is his son!—slumped, dirty, and dragging his feet—but his son all the same. The old man clutches at his chest and gasps at the crisp air. It isn't pain he feels, it's compassion. Gathering his heavy robes into his fists, he breaks and runs across the landscape toward his son. (See Luke 15:11-24.)

When your child has broken trust, you might be tempted to demand an apology, to put him on probation, to make her earn your trust again. But the wisdom of the prodigal's father defies human standards and forgives with scandalous grace. Approach your child with the same kind of grace.

My Daughter,

No matter how many times you mess up, each time you come to Me, I forgive you. My love for you is unconditional. Allow your love for your children to help you let go of the emotions that would cause you to hold on to their mistakes. Just let them go.

Forgiving is one of those areas in which I want you to become as a little child. Have you noticed how quickly they forgive when adults ask for their forgiveness? They don't ask if you've learned your lesson. Their forgiveness seldom depends on how many times you've asked them to forgive you before.

When I forgive, I hurl the offenses into the depths of the sea, forgetting them for all time. As you yield to My love and forgiveness, you will find the grace to do as I do. When you let the hurts go, forgiveness will wash over them, healing your broken heart and restoring your relationships.

Your loving Father

Freedom

Now you are free from the power of sin and are slaves of God,
and his benefits to you include holiness and everlasting life.

ROMANS 6:22 TLB

We know that our old life died with Christ on the cross so that our
sinful selves would have no power over us and we would not be slaves
to sin. Anyone who has died is made free from sin's control.

ROMANS 6:6-7 NCV

The Lord is the Spirit, and where the Spirit of the Lord is,
there is freedom.

2 CORINTHIANS 3:17

Christ has made us free. Now make sure that you stay free
and don't get all tied up again in the chains of slavery to
Jewish laws and ceremonies.

GALATIANS 5:1 TLB

You were called to freedom, brothers and sisters; only do not use
your freedom as an opportunity for self-indulgence, but through
love become slaves to one another.

GALATIANS 5:13 NRSV

Jesus said, "If the Son makes you free, you will be free indeed."

JOHN 8:36 RSV

THE TRUTH WILL SET YOU FREE

Do you remember how free you felt when, having secured a license and a car, you were cut loose to drive? Or how about when you left home for the first time to attend college out of state or to assume independence in your first apartment? Suddenly, there were no curfews, no restrictions concerning what you could watch, who you were with, or what you ate. The first experience of absolute freedom is heady and almost intoxicating.

Oddly enough, with some starts and stops, you finally settled into a routine that demonstrated a high regard for responsibility—to yourself, your family, your values, your country, and society as a whole. How does that happen? And why, for some people, does it fail to occur?

Your heart wrenches to hear the shocking report of a high school classmate whose life ended in a tragic drug overdose. You stare in sobered anguish at the television reporter recounting a case of parental neglect or abuse. You marvel at the news of another robbery, another kidnapping.

As a parent, how can you be sure that your child will not fall into such a lapse of responsibility when it comes to freedom? One critical factor is the knowledge of truth. Jesus said, "You will know the truth, and the truth will set you free" (John 8:32). Children need the truth that is revealed in God's Word, a truth that will take root as they grow in their relationship with Him. Absolute truth acts as an anchor to the soul and fortifies one to take responsibility for his or her existence rather than indulging in self-absorbed living.

Friendship

Accept one another, then, just as Christ accepted you.

ROMANS 15:7

A friend loveth at all times.

PROVERBS 17:17 KJV

As iron sharpens iron, a friend sharpens a friend.

PROVERBS 27:17 NLT

There are "friends" who pretend to be friends,
but there is a friend who sticks closer than a brother.

PROVERBS 18:24 TLB

The eye cannot say to the hand, "I have no need of you," nor again
the head to the feet, "I have no need of you." On the contrary,
the parts of the body which seem to be weaker are indispensable.

1 CORINTHIANS 12:21-22 RSV

Jesus said, "This is my commandment, that you love one another
as I have loved you. No one has greater love than this,
to lay down one's life for one's friends."

JOHN 15:12-13 NRSV

FREE TO BE FRIENDS

"I heard that there's a new girl in your class," Julia said as she drove Bailey to school one rainy morning.

"Nobody likes her, Mom," was Bailey's immediate response.

"Nobody? Not even you?"

"No." At seven years of age, Bailey was a sensitive girl with a strong sense of social acceptance.

"What's her name?" Julia asked.

"Megan. Mom, none of the girls like her, so I can't be her friend."

"I heard that Megan's family moved here to be close to St. Jude's Hospital because her twin sister is very sick."

"She has a twin?"

"They don't look alike right now with the sick sister's hair falling out, you know. Anyway, Megan goes to the hospital every day after school to see her."

"Is she going to die?" Bailey's asked, concerned.

"It's very possible."

"I saw Megan crying yesterday," Bailey's conscience spoke.

"Really?"

Julia pulled up to the curve and leaned over to kiss Bailey's cheek. "Bye, sweetie. See you at 3:15."

"Megan!" Bailey shouted. "Wait up!"

A sad little girl turned to see Bailey bounding up the side-walk with her umbrella, reaching to take Megan under her shelter and into her heart. Julia smiled and drove away.

Given the right information and the freedom to process it in their own way, children will often make very wise choices about friendship, reflecting the values they have learned from your behavior.

Generosity

Let each one [give] as he has made up his own mind and purposed
in his heart, not reluctantly or sorrowfully or under compulsion,
for God loves (He takes pleasure in, prizes above other things, and
is unwilling to abandon or to do without) a cheerful (joyous,
"prompt to do it") giver [whose heart is in his giving].

2 CORINTHIANS 9:7 AMP

Good men will be generous to others
and will be blessed of God for all they do.

ISAIAH 32:8 TLB

You will be enriched in every way for great generosity.

2 CORINTHIANS 9:11 RSV

It is good to be merciful and generous.
Those who are fair in their business will never be defeated.
Good people will always be remembered.

PSALM 112:5-6 NCV

A generous man will prosper;
he who refreshes others will himself be refreshed.

PROVERBS 11:25

Heavenly Father:

I admit, sometimes I find it hard to give. I want to be generous with others, but after I've spent the entire day laying my life down for my family and taking care of all my responsibilities, I feel that there is very little left over to offer others. I certainly don't want to be stingy or selfish with my time, my energy, or my finances, because that is the opposite of Your nature. Your generosity never ceases; I want to be like You.

Make me aware of opportunities where I can do something to make a difference. Whether it is donating canned goods to a food drive or simply helping an elderly person carry her packages into the post office, show me ways in which I can be generous with others and allow Your love to flow through me. Thank You for helping me to become the "cheerful giver" whom Your Word says You love.

Amen.

RECKLESS GIVING

For most people, the problem with generosity is that it costs too much—too much money, too much time, too much inconvenience, too much sacrifice. True generosity pours from the heart without caution or measure.

A mother pulled a plate of frosted brownies out of the pantry, preparing to serve them to her family. Her mouth watered as she carefully lifted each piece from the dish and onto a plate. Her young daughter stood at her elbow watching.

"Mama," the girl suddenly exclaimed, "there are only four brownies, but five of us."

"I'm not really hungry for chocolate," Mama hurried to answer.

Content with her reply, the youngster enthusiastically helped distribute the delicacy. Thirty years later, the scene repeats itself with the little girl playing the unselfish role of Mama, and the legacy of the generous heart continues.

My Daughter,

Giving is an amazing thing. The more you bestow on others, the more you receive yourself. But I don't want that to be your primary motive. Nonetheless, I established a spiritual law of sowing and reaping—whatever you sow, that shall you reap. When you give with the right motives, eventually blessings come back to you.

For love's sake, I gave My one and only Son, knowing that I would reap many children in return. I was separated from My creation, but the gift of My beloved Son and His willingness to sacrifice His own life brought many sons and daughters into My kingdom and presence. This generous gift gave you the right to call Me Father. I gave a Son, and I received many more sons and daughters.

When you love, you give. As you grow more interested in the success of others, it will motivate you to help them pursue their destiny. In return, you'll find that you discover your own.

Your loving Father

Gentleness

The wisdom that comes from heaven is first of all
pure and full of quiet gentleness.

JAMES 3:17 TLB

My friends, if anyone is detected in a transgression,
you who have received the Spirit should restore such a one in a spirit
of gentleness. Take care that you yourselves are not tempted.

GALATIANS 6:1 NRSV

A gentle answer turns away wrath, but harsh words cause quarrels.

PROVERBS 15:1 TLB

The Lord's servants must not quarrel but must be kind to everyone.
They must be . . . patient with difficult people. They should gently
teach those who oppose the truth. Perhaps God will change those
people's hearts, and they will believe the truth. Then they will come
to their senses and escape from the Devil's trap.

2 TIMOTHY 2:24-26 NLT

Jesus said, "God blesses those who are gentle and lowly,
for the whole earth will belong to them."

MATTHEW 5:5 NLT

GENTLEMEN FROM
GENTLE WOMEN

A high school student on his way home from school caught sight of a little girl standing beside her bicycle crying. He pulled up and asked from inside the car, "What's the matter?"

"My dress is caught," she bawled.

Sure enough, the hem of her dress had gotten caught between the chain and the gear. Black grease had left a brutal smudge on the pink gingham fabric.

"Where's your mom?" he called back.

"She's with my baby brother," she wailed.

The young man opened the door and made his way to the little girl's side where he began trying to extract the dress from the bicycle's metal teeth.

"What do you think you are doing?" a woman screamed as she ran from the porch two doors down.

"Huh?" the teenage boy stammered. "Oh, is this your daughter? Sorry, ma'am, her dress is caught in her bike and I'm trying to get it out."

Calming down, the woman asked, "Are you okay, honey?"

"My dress is caught," she answered.

"There!" the boy announced triumphantly.

"Thank you so much," the girl's mother responded. "I'm sorry I yelled at you. I just didn't know . . ."

"Hey, these days you can't be too careful," he nodded, getting back into his car.

"Wait."

"Yes?"

"I don't know many guys your age who would care enough about a little girl's tears to take the time to stop. Thank you."

He grinned. "I guess my mama raised me right!"

God's Faithfulness

All the paths of the Lord are steadfast love and faithfulness,
for those who keep his covenant and his testimonies.

PSALM 25:10 RSV

Your love, O Lord, reaches to the heavens,
your faithfulness to the skies.

PSALM 36:5

Great is his steadfast love toward us;
and the faithfulness of the Lord endures for ever.

PSALM 117:2 RSV

I face your Temple as I worship, giving thanks to you for
all your lovingkindness and your faithfulness, for your promises are
backed by all the honor of your name.

PSALM 138:2 TLB

Lord, you are a God who shows mercy and is kind.
You don't become angry quickly.
You have great love and faithfulness.

PSALM 86:15 NCV

FAITHFUL IN LOVE

"Excuse me," Shelley said to the woman. "What happened to your son?"

Shelley had seen her from across the waiting room as she entered, holding the boy like an infant. His head dangled down over her arm at an angle with which they were both accustomed. The boy's eyes stared off into nothingness, his left arm flailing spontaneously from time to time.

"He almost drowned when he was three," she answered. "He is eight now."

"Five years?" Shelley touched his forehead with her palm, compassion flooding her heart.

"I've been all over the country trying to find someone who could heal him," she continued. "We are about out of options."

"Have you seen this doctor before?" Shelley was a "walk-in" as she was new in town.

"Yes, he is our regular physician. But last week we were in New Orleans consulting with a specialist."

Shelley probed. "What did he say?"

"He said there's nothing we can do for Samuel but pray." Tears rolled from her eyes and down her cheeks. "I've been praying for five years, but there's been no answer."

Shelley felt her own eyes fill with tears, and she couldn't help reaching out to touch the boy's cheek with her fingertips.

"Your mother takes good care of you, doesn't she, Samuel?" She looked up at the woman and said softly, "I know it's not what you want, but maybe you are Samuel's answer. At least, I see the faithfulness of God in the way you love your son. Thank you for showing me that."

God's faithfulness is demonstrated not merely in the answers we want, but in the way we love.

God's Love

God shows his great love for us in this way:
Christ died for us while we were still sinners.

ROMANS 5:8 NCV

The Lord shows mercy and is kind.
He does not become angry quickly, and he has great love.

PSALM 103:8 NCV

The Lord passed in front of Moses and said, "I am the Lord.
The Lord is a God who shows mercy, who is kind, who doesn't
become angry quickly, who has great love and faithfulness and
is kind to thousands of people. The Lord forgives people for evil,
for sin, and for turning against him."

EXODUS 34:6-7 NCV

They refused to listen;
they forgot the miracles you did for them.
So they became stubborn and turned against you,
choosing a leader to take them back to slavery.
But you are a forgiving God. You are kind and full of mercy.
You do not become angry quickly, and you have great love.
So you did not leave them.

NEHEMIAH 9:17 NCV

Heavenly Father:

The most outstanding attribute of Your character is that You are love. More than anything, I want to have, and I want my children to have, a revelation of how much You love us—personally and individually.

At times, their faith is so much stronger than mine and their relationship with You seems to come much easier to them than it does to me. When they say things to You and about You that seem silly to my adult mind, I'm tempted to correct them. I know it's my job to teach them about You, but help me to realize that I don't have to understand their way of communicating with You. I just need to be thankful that they are listening and that You are meeting them where they are.

Help me to always have an open ear to their questions and to respond by Your leading. That way I can help them grow closer to You.

And, Father, help me to receive from You as easily as my children do—ever looking, ever listening for what You have to say to me.

Amen.

GOD'S LOVE SPEAKS

"Mommy," four-year-old C.J. quavered as he woke his mother. He was in her bed, so she could monitor his fever.

"Where did Daddy go?" the tiny voice continued.

She reached to touch his cheek. "He's at his house, baby."

"No, he's not. He was talking to me just now."

"You must have been dreaming," she frowned, tears welling up in her eyes. Three months ago Lee had moved out, and C.J. was having great difficulty adjusting to his parents' separation.

"No, Mommy, it wasn't a dream. He was talking to me."

"Well, what did he say?" Kacie played along, hoping to keep him from getting upset in the middle of the night.

"He said, 'Don't worry.'"

"Were you worried?"

"I'm scared you might leave me."

"Oh, baby, I will never leave you," she said as she hugged him in a tight embrace, rocking him gently in her arms.

"Mommy?" C.J.'s quivering voice interrupted the quiet sobs again. "You were right; it wasn't Daddy."

"So it was a dream, after all?" She felt relieved.

"No, I wasn't asleep," he said, sniffing back his tears.

"What was it then?" Suddenly, she was confused.

"It was God talking," he sighed.

Silence passed peacefully between them, and as C.J. fell asleep in her arms, Kacie lay still, listening with a grateful heart for the voice her son had heard.

God speaks in ways that are as varied as the people to whom He speaks. A wise mother will encourage her children to always be listening for His voice as they develop their individual walks with Him.

My Daughter,

More than anything else, I want all people to know how very much I love them. It is why I sent My Son to pay for all their shortcomings and mistakes. Children often find it easier to receive My love than adults do because they have less of life's garbage in their minds from the disappointment that life's trials can bring.

That's one reason Jesus called the little children to come to Him when the disciples told them to leave Him alone. In the children, He found hearts ready to trust and love Him, ready to believe His new way of life.

Like your children take My love at face value, you are to do the same. Realize that I will do everything in My power to help you succeed. I love you unconditionally!

Your loving Father

God's Will

We have not ceased praying for you and asking that
you may be filled with the knowledge of God's will
in all spiritual wisdom and understanding.

COLOSSIANS 1:9 NRSV

Do not conform any longer to the pattern of this world,
but be transformed by the renewing of your mind.
Then you will be able to test and approve what God's will is—
his good, pleasing and perfect will.

ROMANS 12:2

The Holy Spirit helps us with our daily problems and in our
praying. For we don't even know what we should pray for,
nor how to pray as we should; but the Holy Spirit . . .
pleads for us in harmony with God's own will.

ROMANS 8:26-27 TLB

Jesus said, "Take my yoke upon you, and learn from me;
for I am gentle and humble in heart, and you will find rest for your
souls. For my yoke is easy, and my burden is light."

MATTHEW 11:29-30 NRSV

Jesus said, "Anyone who does God's will is my brother,
and my sister, and my mother."

MARK 3:35 TLB

KNOWING GOD'S WILL

Mothers talk about seeking God's will for their children, frequently falling to the temptation of imposing their own will instead. And though a mom's motive may be pure, this may prove to be her greatest downfall in effective parenting.

There is a very simple formula in the Bible that will help you to avoid that fatal flaw. The key lies in discerning what the will of God is for you, leaving the discovery of His will for your children between Him and them.

Paul wrote with great insight into God's will for you as a mom. First he said, "Always be joyful" (1 Thessalonians 5:16 TLB). Being joyful as a mother involves a great deal of discipline. Small irritations grate on you all day, not to mention moments of true crisis. Babies cry, toddlers fall, teenagers rebel, milk gets spilled, lies get told, and feelings get hurt. The key to joy lies not in your circumstances, but in your relationship with God—in the depths of your heart, rather than in what happens throughout the day. Make it a habit to rejoice in your children so they will be free to discover who they are and what their purpose is.

Second, God's will for you includes prayer. "Keep on praying" (v. 17). Time spent fuming is time wasted. Invest your emotional energy in prayer, rather than in worrying. You will discover that God's willingness to act in support of your children will give you great relief and comfort. And your confidence in His power will translate to your children.

Finally, "no matter what happens, always be thankful" (v. 18). This is the greatest challenge of all. Master it!

God's Word

Your word is a lamp for my feet
and a light for my path.

PSALM 119:105 NLT

Your words are what sustain me; they are food to my hungry soul.
They bring joy to my sorrowing heart and delight me.

JEREMIAH 15:16 TLB

The Word that God speaks is alive and full of power [making it
active, operative, energizing, and effective]; it is sharper than any
two-edged sword, penetrating to the dividing line of the breath of
life . . . and . . . spirit, and . . . [of the deepest parts of our nature],
exposing and sifting and analyzing and judging the very thoughts
and purposes of the heart.

HEBREWS 4:12 AMP

The Word became flesh and made his dwelling among us.
We have seen his glory, the glory of the One and Only,
who came from the Father, full of grace and truth.

JOHN 1:14

I treasure your word in my heart,
so that I may not sin against you.

PSALM 119:11 NRSV

GOD'S WORD CHANGES THINGS

"Jairus, please go talk to that Healer," she had said to her husband early in the week when their twelve-year-old daughter had suddenly fallen ill.

"You know I can't take that risk, dear," he had responded. "Yesterday I heard about a synagogue leader near Cana who had lost favor with the Rabbi because he went public in support of Jesus."

Jairus was a prominent man. He led synagogue worship and fraternized with religious dignitaries. His wife understood why they couldn't admit to their faith in Jesus. But when their daughter got sick and the fever persisted for four days, all she really cared about was getting help.

Yesterday, it had all come to a head.

"Jairus, please go get the Miracle-worker. Phoebe is dying."

Jairus recognized his wife's intuitive dread and set out to find Jesus.

The hours crawled across the tortured day until, finally, Jairus returned with Him to find his wife sobbing on the cot where the dead child rested in her desperate embrace.

The Healer reached for the limp hand of the little girl and examined her delicate fingers, tracing the lines of her palm with His forefinger, admiring His Father's work.

That was when He drew the breath with which He exhaled these words: "Get up, little girl!" (Mark 5:41 NLT).

As if merely stirred from a nap, she did precisely as He commanded!

God's Word, as found in the Bible, always has a striking impact. You can rely on its truth and witness circumstances change. It will empower you to be the best mother you can be.

Goodness

If you are wise and understand God's ways, live a life of steady goodness so that only good deeds will pour forth.

JAMES 3:13 NLT

You were made free from sin, and now you are slaves to goodness.

ROMANS 6:18 NCV

Whenever you are able,
do good to people who need help.

PROVERBS 3:27 NCV

The Kingdom of God is not a matter of what we eat or drink, but of living a life of goodness and peace and joy in the Holy Spirit. If you serve Christ with this attitude, you will please God.

ROMANS 14:17-18 NLT

In the past you were full of darkness, but now you are full of light in the Lord. So live like children who belong to the light. Light brings every kind of goodness, right living, and truth.

EPHESIANS 5:8-9 NCV

Heavenly Father:

God, You are so good, and everything You have created is good. Now that I think about it, that must mean that You created me to be good too. And because You live in me Your goodness must live in me as well.

I want this goodness to be evident to everyone who comes across my path. When I'm tired at the end of the day, though, it can be hard to respond to my family that way. It takes Your grace.

Today I choose for Your goodness to become more apparent in me. Help me to respond to others in a way that they see all the things that make life rich, vibrant, and wonderful. As they see that I'm becoming more and more the goodness-filled person You created me to be, I want them to see You as the good God You really are.

Amen.

GOODNESS IS OF GOD

Corinne often recalled her mother's voice: "Be good, Corrie, for goodness is of God."

Years later, Corinne discovered in the Scriptures that a man had addressed Jesus as "Good Teacher" (Mark 10:17 TLB). She thought the Lord's response was very peculiar and a little misleading: "Why do you call me good? Only God is truly good!" (v. 18). She wondered, *Wasn't Jesus good too?*

Now that her own children were running down hallways, bumping into tables, tipping over lamps, Corinne found herself saying over and over, "Be good, kids. Please be good." Yet because of her misunderstanding of what Jesus said, she refused to end with her mother's admonition: "For goodness is of God."

That is, until Michael slammed the front door on Tim's finger. Rushing him to the emergency room, Corinne was relieved that her mother could help her in transit.

Nine stitches later, Corinne walked up behind her mother in the waiting room as her conversation with Michael was coming to its conclusion.

"So goodness, Michael, covers just about everything—even not slamming doors when you're mad at your brother."

Corinne cut into the conversation. "Hey, Mom, do you remember that verse in Mark when Jesus says that only God can be good? If even Jesus said that, what chance have we got?"

"That wasn't what He meant! He meant that whatever goodness we see in people is evidence that God is present!" explained her mother.

"What about in me?" Michael's finger jabbed his chest.

"Oh, yes, Michael," she smiled broadly. "Especially in you."

"That makes me feel good," Michael said as he grinned sheepishly.

"See! That's what I'm talking about!" She whisked him into her arms and hugged him tight.

My Daughter,

You are right. When I created your world, I looked upon it and said, "It is good!" I am life and I created life to be good. And you are My creation—the work of My very own hands. Yes, you are good too!

I have already filled you with My goodness. All that I am resides in you because you are My child, but you have to open up the well of life within you and allow that goodness to flow out.

You have asked Me to help you show My goodness to those around you, and this blesses My heart. Be encouraged—as you let your light shine, You are becoming more and more like Me every single day!

Your loving Father

Grace

The amazing grace of the Master, Jesus Christ,
the extravagant love of God, the intimate friendship
of the Holy Spirit, be with all of you.

2 CORINTHIANS 13:14 MSG

If your life honors the name of Jesus, he will honor you.
Grace is behind and through all of this, our God giving himself
freely, the Master, Jesus Christ, giving himself freely.

2 THESSALONIANS 1:12 MSG

Now God has us where he wants us, with all the time in this world
and the next to shower grace and kindness upon us in Christ Jesus.

EPHESIANS 2:7 MSG

From his fullness we have all received, grace upon grace.
The law indeed was given through Moses; grace and truth came
through Jesus Christ.

JOHN 1:16-17 NRSV

Even though on the outside it often looks like things are falling
apart on us, on the inside, where God is making new life,
not a day goes by without his unfolding grace.

2 CORINTHIANS 4:16 MSG

AMAZING GRACE,
HOW SWEET THE SOUND

A classic hymn brings to mind a concept worth considering. Ask yourself these questions as you reflect on some familiar phrases:

Amazing Grace, how sweet the sound . . . Do you have a warm and vibrant understanding of grace? Are your children witnesses of the way you lavish it upon others?

That saved a wretch like me . . . Do you give grace as abundantly as you have received it?

I once was lost, but now I'm found . . . Do you have compassion on those who don't yet know God's grace? The unkind and inconsiderate?

Was blind, but now I see . . . Do you remember how short-sighted you were before you discovered the meaning of grace? Do your words and actions bear evidence that you now have a gracious perspective?

'Twas grace that taught my heart to fear . . . Do you honor God in such a way that your children are learning to respect Him?

And grace my fears relieved . . . Do you speak of Him and to Him in ways that communicate to your children how much you trust Him?

How precious did that grace appear . . . Do your children understand how much value you place on God's grace?

The hour I first believed. Do your children recognize faith in you?

Consider teaching your child this famous old hymn, and take the opportunity to commit together to a gracious standard of living.

Grief

Surely He has borne our griefs
And carried our sorrows; . . .
And by His stripes we are healed.
ISAIAH 53:4-5 NKJV

Jesus said, "Very truly, I tell you, you will weep and mourn,
but the world will rejoice; you will have pain, but your pain
will turn into joy."
JOHN 16:20 NRSV

The Lord is close to the brokenhearted
and saves those who are crushed in spirit.
PSALM 34:18

He will not break the bruised reed, nor quench the
dimly burning flame. He will encourage the fainthearted,
those tempted to despair.
ISAIAH 42:3 TLB

Jesus said, "Blessed are those who mourn,
for they shall be comforted."
MATTHEW 5:4 NKJV

HEARTACHE THAT LINGERS

Climbing a tree in her front yard, eight-year-old Melissa watched as her beloved dog, Fannie, was struck by a car. Brakes squealing, metal hitting flesh, and Fannie's dying yelp all combined to impress deep, painful scars into Melissa's memory. Worst of all was the sight of the bloody, mangled pet on the curb directly beneath her.

From the day the family had brought Fannie home as a puppy, she had slept at the foot of Melissa's bed and had accompanied her everywhere she went. In fact, Fannie's misfortunate end was the result of her distress over Melissa's climb. Watching from the base of the tree, she had edged into the street to keep her in view.

It took several weeks for Melissa to recuperate from the trauma of Fannie's violent death. She felt agonizing guilt over having been where Fannie couldn't follow, and her heartache lingered.

Melissa's mother encouraged her to talk about everything she experienced the day Fannie died. "What did you hear? What did you see? What did you feel?" For many days after, she inquired: "What are you thinking about?" taking the time to discuss Melissa's grief every time she encountered it.

Finally, after a few weeks she announced, "Today we're going to pick out a new puppy!"

"We can't!" Melissa protested. "Fannie would be hurt."

"No," her mother assured her, "the greatest compliment we can pay Fannie is that because of her, we simply can't live without a dog!"

Your children will experience grief for a variety of reasons, and they will need assistance in dealing with the feelings associated with it. A vital part of the process is learning that life must go on, but as it does, Jesus will heal the broken heart.

Guidance

Remember those who led you, who spoke the word of God to you;
and considering the result of their conduct, imitate their faith.

HEBREWS 13:7 NASB

Beloved, do not imitate what is evil, but what is good.
The one who does good is of God;
the one who does evil has not seen God.

3 JOHN 1:11 NASB

We do not want you to become lazy, but to imitate those who
through faith and patience inherit what has been promised.

HEBREWS 6:12

The apostle Paul wrote, "I urge you, imitate me.
For this reason I have sent Timothy to you, who is my beloved
and faithful son in the Lord, who will remind you
of my ways in Christ."

1 CORINTHIANS 4:16-17 NKJV

Follow God's example in everything you do
just as a much loved child imitates his father.

EPHESIANS 5:1 TLB

Heavenly Father:

I primarily receive guidance from Your Word, but You also use people. I ask You to bring godly mentors into my life who have walked the road I am walking now. Help me to recognize mothers who excel in their relationship with their children; who have been successful in disciplining, teaching, and guiding their children; and who have had a dynamic spiritual impact on them.

Some of these women I can learn from by observation, but I also need one or two veteran moms to whom I can bare my soul—women with whom I can be transparent, who will help answer my questions, and who I know will pray for me and encourage my faith.

Thank You for placing these special women in my life. As I freely receive of their wisdom, I will be faithful to pass it on to others.

Amen.

IMITATING THOSE YOU ADMIRE

The apostle Paul wrote, "Be imitators of me, just as I also am of Christ" (I Corinthians 11:1 NASB).

Now, there's some good advice! When you are in need of guidance, choose someone in your midst who models the outcome you desire, and pay attention to how they got there.

The writer of Proverbs challenges his readers: "Ears to hear and eyes to see—both are gifts from the Lord" (20:12 NLT). Listening and observation are our best resources for gathering information that will contribute to having fulfilling relationships.

Be observant. Develop the habit of noticing women who have exceptional relationships with their children. Be selective. Choose someone who has maintained a high level of intimacy and influence with her children throughout their childhood and into adulthood. Are her children the kind of people you admire? Does her life and the lives of her children reflect the values you cherish?

If the answer is yes, then pay attention to the distinctive qualities about her that lend themselves toward your own goals in mothering. Is she particularly expressive, demonstrative, quiet, responsive, gentle, patient, or cheerful? You'll begin to notice things about her that should tip you off to her effectiveness.

Listen carefully. Next, listen in on her interaction with others, particularly with her children. What is her communication style? Is she talkative or reserved? Does she ask questions? Does she make comments? How is her conversation with others unique?

Though it might strike you as elementary, choosing a mentor is an effective means of receiving good guidance. The key is to find someone you admire. The goal is to become such an individual.

My Daughter,

Paul said, "Follow me as I follow Christ." There is great benefit in modeling your life after those who have already successfully maneuvered the difficulties of motherhood. Instead of having to find your way on your own, you can follow the lead of those who have gone before you.

All the relationships I bring into your life are treasures, but not every person is role-model material. Listen for My voice among the many voices surrounding you. You can locate qualified mentors by the words they speak. When their words sound like My Word, you can trust their wise counsel. When their lives are filled with positive actions and an abundance of spiritual fruit, you can follow their example with confidence.

As you glean wisdom from the lives of successful mothers, I will help you incorporate that wisdom into your own life. I will show you how their guidance fits into My plan for you and your children.

Your loving Father

Guilt

There was a time when I wouldn't admit what a sinner I was.
But my dishonesty made me miserable and filled my days
with frustration. All day and all night your hand was heavy on me.
My strength evaporated like water on a sunny day until I finally
admitted all my sins to you and stopped trying to hide them.
I said to myself, "I will confess them to the Lord."
And you forgave me! All my guilt is gone.

PSALM 32:3-5 TLB

As far as the east is from the west,
so far has he removed our transgressions from us.

PSALM 103:12

What happiness for those whose guilt has been forgiven!
What joys when sins are covered over! What relief for those who
have confessed their sins and God has cleared their record.

PSALM 32:1-2 TLB

If we claim to be without sin, we deceive ourselves and the truth is
not in us. If we confess our sins, he is faithful and just and will
forgive us our sins and purify us from all unrighteousness.

1 JOHN 1:8-9

THE GOOD NEWS ABOUT GUILT

Guilt is typically dealt with in a negative frame of reference, but here is some good news:

- Feeling guilt is normal. All people experience guilt—if they are normal, that is. The only alternative is an absence of conscience, which when taken to extremes means psychopathic tendencies. The next time you feel a pang of conscience, be thankful you have one.
- Feeling guilt is necessary. When your conscience stings, it is raising a red flag, alerting you that something is wrong and needs appropriate attention.
- Feeling guilt is healthy. Your response to guilt will determine your emotional welfare, as well as the condition of your relationships and spiritual well-being. The following suggestions will keep guilt from becoming an unhealthy issue:
  1. Admit to yourself what you did.
  2. Confess to God—and others, if you have violated a relationship. Have spiritual and relational integrity.
  3. Make restitution if there is anything within reason you can do to make amends.
  4. Make a commitment to yourself and, if necessary, to others, reinforcing your relationships with your word.
  5. Keep your promise to yourself no matter what temptation arises. Do not compromise or bargain with your conscience.
  6. Get past it and get on with living. Browbeating yourself won't benefit anyone. You have to be as willing to forgive yourself as you are willing to forgive others.

As you incorporate healthy ways of dealing with guilt into your own life, your children will gain valuable tools with which to deal with it themselves.

Hope

Don't worry about anything; instead, pray about everything;
tell God your needs, and don't forget to thank him for his answers.
If you do this you will experience God's peace, which is far more
wonderful than the human mind can understand.
His peace will keep your thoughts and your hearts quiet and
at rest as you trust in Christ Jesus.

PHILIPPIANS 4:6-7 TLB

May the God of hope fill you with all joy and peace in believing, so
that by the power of the Holy Spirit you may abound in hope.

ROMANS 15:13 RSV

The Lord is good to those whose hope is in him,
to the one who seeks him.

LAMENTATIONS 3:25

Be strong and take courage,
all you who put your hope in the Lord!

PSALM 31:24 NLT

The hope of the righteous ends in gladness.

PROVERBS 10:28 RSV

COUNTING PORCUPINES INSTEAD OF SHEEP

If you lie awake at night feeling hopeless anxiety over the condition of the world, the stress of finances, your child's grades, or the rebellion you sense in your teenager, you might want to add to your list the threat of a porcupine invasion.

Here is a list of things to fret over since you're awake anyway:

Did you know that porcupines are rodents, defending themselves by thrashing barbed tails?

Furthermore, their quills detach easily, sticking into their victim's flesh. These quills are actually bristles of hair that have fused together—sort of like dreadlocks with a deadly dose of hair spray. Some have backward-pointing barbs on the tip, which hook into your flesh and are almost impossible to remove—if you survive. You can die from infection caused by germs on a porcupine's quills or from damage done to a vital organ. So if you are going to lie awake feeling hopeless, you might as well add the threat of porcupines to your list of reasons to despair.

However, if you prefer to turn your mind to brighter thoughts, there is some good news. Porcupines don't prefer the habitations of humans; they hang around in trees. Porcupines don't go looking for trouble either. In fact, they'd rather spend their time munching bark. And the best news of all is that they cannot shoot their quills like you've seen on animated television shows.

Sound facetious? Most of the things over which we worry are as likely to happen as a porcupine invasion. There is more reason to hope than to despair. Practice the uplifting experience of hope, beginning with reasons to believe that you won't be attacked by a porcupine.

Humility

Toward the scorners he is scornful,
but to the humble he shows favor.

PROVERBS 3:34 NRSV

All who humble themselves before the Lord shall be given
every blessing, and shall have wonderful peace.

PSALM 37:11 TLB

I say, through the grace given unto me, to every man
that is among you, not to think of himself more highly than he
ought to think; but to think soberly, according as God hath dealt
to every man the measure of faith.

ROMANS 12:3 KJV

Humble yourselves before the Lord and he will exalt you.

JAMES 4:10 RSV

All of you serve each other with humble spirits, for God gives special
blessings to those who are humble, but sets himself against those
who are proud. If you will humble yourselves under the mighty
hand of God, in his good time he will lift you up.

1 PETER 5:5-6 TLB

Heavenly Father:

As my children grow, they become less and less dependent on me, and sometimes that is hard. I want them to stand on their own, but recognizing that our relationship is changing affects my emotions and actions.

Sometimes it hurts me to see that they don't need me like they used to. Help me to see that their independence doesn't make me less of a mother—it just means they need me on a different level with each stage of growth. Give me wisdom to know how to let go when they're ready. Teach me to embrace their maturity, and show us how to begin relating to each other as brothers and sisters in Christ as they move into adulthood.

Thank You for the relationship I have with them. Help me to be the mother they need for every stage of their lives.

Amen.

HE MUST INCREASE,
I MUST DECREASE

As many as one-and-a-half million people flocked to John the Baptist in the wilderness to hear him preach, including a powerful group of Israel's religious dignitaries.

"Who are you?" they inquired. "Are you the One we've been waiting for?" The sheer number of respondents impressed them, especially since John the Baptist hadn't been ordained through any of their schools.

"I am not the One," he confessed. "A man can receive nothing unless it has been given him from heaven. My job is to bear witness to the One who is coming. He must increase, but I must decrease." (See John 3:23-30.)

John the Baptist demonstrated true humility when resisting the temptation to seize the opportunity for his own advantage. Instead, he publicly deferred to the mission of Jesus. He understood his own mission and knew his place. It is a noble thing to accept when it is your job to move over and allow someone else to take the reins.

When rearing children, it is in their best interest—as well as your own—to keep in mind that one day they must increase, and you must decrease. Moms work so diligently to nurture their relationships with their young throughout adolescence. If they aren't careful, however, they can unwittingly demolish what they've built when they refuse to let their children take control of their own lives and futures once adulthood is reached.

You might be tempted to rationalize, saying, "I want only what's best for my children." But they may interpret your efforts as imposing and controlling. Humility is realizing when it is time for your relationship to change. It is the risky business of letting go, trusting your child to step up to the plate and hit a home run.

My Daughter,

Letting go of your children as they grow is never easy, but you have the right idea. I applaud your willingness to adjust and change as they mature.

All these years I've entrusted you to bring them up in My ways so they can fulfill the potential I've placed within them. Now it's your turn to trust Me. Place them into My capable hands. I know their dreams as well as I know the dreams you have for them. As they've followed you in obedience, now they're ready to take a bigger step and follow Me.

Instead of seeing yourself letting go, imagine taking the hands that you've held all this time and placing them into Mine. You've brought them this far . . . now I'll take over to guide them on their journey. You can trust Me.

Your loving Father

Identity

Jesus said, "You are the light that gives light to the world. . . .
Live so that they will see the good things you do and
will praise your Father in heaven."
MATTHEW 5:14,16 NCV

You are a people set apart as holy to God, your God. God,
your God, chose you out of all the people on Earth for himself
as a cherished, personal treasure.
DEUTERONOMY 7:6 MSG

You are a chosen people, a royal priesthood, a holy nation, a people
belonging to God, that you may declare the praises of him who
called you out of darkness into his wonderful light.
1 PETER 2:9

Thus says the Lord,
he who created you, O Jacob,
he who formed you, O Israel:
"Fear not, for I have redeemed you;
I have called you by name, you are mine."
ISAIAH 43:1 RSV

Jesus said, "You didn't choose me! I chose you! I appointed you to
go and produce lovely fruit always."
JOHN 15:16 TLB

A NEW NAME

Andrew ran to tell his brother Simon about the Lord. "We have found the One about whom the Scriptures testify," he said.

Simon agreed to investigate the situation.

Looking intently at him, Jesus said, "You are Simon, the son of Jonah; you shall be called [Peter]" (John 1:42 NKJV).

Consider these profound implications concerning identity:

- Simon's original identity was given him by his parents. As a parent, you have had the privilege of providing a name and a heritage for your children.

- Simon's identity linked him to his family in a particular way—as the son of Jonah. While small, your children's primary function is to serve the family's mission and preserve the family's heritage.

- Jesus acknowledged Simon's original identity. The Lord sanctions the provision that parents make in nurturing children with a sense of individuality and a commitment to family.

- Jesus changed Simon's identity. There comes a time in the lives of children when they must answer to a higher calling—something that reaches beyond the parameters of family—a larger vision.

- Simon's new identity reframed his relationships with family and society. Their new identity will require your children to reevaluate their responsibilities and goals and to reexamine their priorities to determine who they are and what they are called to do.

Integrity demands that the child's identity answer to what he is gifted and equipped to offer to the world. A wise mother will respect that the sovereignty of God will take over where she leaves off once the little boy becomes a man and the girl becomes a woman.

Integrity

I will be careful to live a blameless life— . . .
I will lead a life of integrity
in my own home.
PSALM 101:2 NLT

Happy are people of integrity,
who follow the law of the Lord. . . .
They do not compromise with evil,
and they walk only in His paths.
PSALM 119:1,3 NLT

Jesus said, "You are a good and loyal servant.
Because you were loyal with small things, I will let you care for much
greater things. Come and share my joy with me."
MATTHEW 25:21 NCV

To the faithful you show yourself faithful;
to those with integrity you show integrity.
PSALM 18:25 NLT

The Lord does not look at the things man looks at.
Man looks at the outward appearance,
but the Lord looks at the heart.
1 SAMUEL 16:7

SIMPLY A REFLECTION

"It's not my fault that they sent two," Sharon laughed, talking into the receiver. "Besides, no one will ever know that I didn't pay for it."

Her son Sam was eating his breakfast within earshot of the phone conversation. His gaze made Sharon squirm and she turned her back to finish.

"Won't Karen be impressed when Sam shows up with a sixty-dollar video game at Casen's birthday party?"

Karen was the envy of the neighborhood. She lived in the finest house, drove the newest SUV, had a custom-made pool, wore designer clothes, and always sent Casen to birthday parties with expensive, impressive gifts. No one outshone Casen. Consequently, he was the most popular kid on the block.

The day of the party, Sharon walked Sam to Casen's house. Though at five Sam was the youngest child there, he was sure to rise in Casen's eyes when the gifts were unwrapped.

A phone call came after the party.

"Sharon," Beth's voice had an urgent tone. "I thought I should warn you . . ."

"What?" she felt the blood rush from her face.

"I stayed to help Karen with the party. When Casen opened Sam's gift, he was delighted."

Sharon beamed. This was just the report she had hoped to hear.

"But things went south when Karen said to Sam, 'Your mommy spent far too much on Casen, Sam.'"

"Why, what happened?"

"Sam said, 'Don't worry, Mommy didn't pay for that one. They accidentally sent two in the mail.'"

As a mother, you are responsible to model integrity for your children. Oftentimes, unwittingly, they simply mirror what they see in you—be it good or bad. Live so that they reflect right living.

Joy

Keep your eyes on Jesus, our leader and instructor.
He was willing to die a shameful death on the cross because of the
joy he knew would be his afterwards; and now he sits
in the place of honor by the throne of God.

HEBREWS 12:2 TLB

Count it all joy when you fall into various trials,
knowing that the testing of your faith produces patience.
But let patience have its perfect work, that you may be perfect
and complete, lacking nothing.

JAMES 1:2-4 NKJV

Weeping may endure for a night,
But joy comes in the morning.

PSALM 30:5 NKJV

Be full of joy in the Lord always. I will say again, be full of joy.

PHILIPPIANS 4:4 NCV

Jesus said, "Until now you have asked nothing in My name.
Ask, and you will receive, that your joy may be full."

JOHN 16:24 NKJV

Heavenly Father:

My children's antics can so grate on my nerves. The constant bouncing, running, and high level of energy is sometimes too much—no matter how big the house. And the questions! Answering "why" forty-seven times a day wears on my mind. I thought it would get easier as they grew up, but the teenage years bring their own set of challenges.

I don't want to gripe and complain. My children are truly the light of my life, but motherhood is harder than I thought it would be. Help me to change my perspective. I want to see joy in the little things they do. Teach me to find a funnier side of life, and help me to be lighthearted and filled with joy. Show me how to choose my words wisely and not take everything so seriously. Let my children see Your heart in me.

Amen.

FORGETTING THE PAIN

There is a wise philosophy tucked into a discourse Jesus had with His friends concerning joy. He said, "When your kids put you through really tough times, even through excruciating pain, just remember that you will have great joy in whom they are to become!"

Okay, maybe that isn't exactly what He said. But let it sink in and you'll discover that it goes a long way to help you keep your perspective during trying times. For instance . . .

Two-year-old Kate tips over her bowl of cereal because she won't stay seated like her mom said. The spilled milk stains the upholstery and stirs her mother's ire. Kate's energy, which irritates her mother now, will be a tremendous asset when, at twenty-four, she becomes a fourth-grade teacher.

Twelve-year-old Troy drives his mother to the edge of insanity with his constant thumping—on the table, the oatmeal box, the shower door, and even drumming on his dinner plate with a fork and spoon, chipping her fine china. The rhythm which today mars the plate—and his mother's mood—will be a great blessing to many when at thirty he becomes the drummer in the praise band at church.

And even when defiance or rebellion plagues your relationship like a cloud of gloom, don't give up, for the strength of spirit demonstrated during a child's immaturity may be forecasting the uncommon courage of tomorrow's hero.

So what was it Jesus really said? "A woman giving birth to a child has pain because her time has come; but when her baby is born she forgets the anguish because of her joy that a child is born into the world" (John 16:21).

My Daughter,

I realize that motherhood is fraught with frustration, but it is also filled with incredible joy.

It's easy to focus on the wrong actions of your children when they disobey and bicker, and to a point, this is necessary in order to administer discipline. But once you've taken care of business, determine to look beyond the frustrations and focus on My ultimate plan for them. You'll find that you can more easily let go of the negative emotions and be filled with My joy once again.

Parenting is indeed serious business, but I don't want you to get bogged down. Lighten up! Laugh and have fun with your kids! Live each moment to the fullest and be filled with My joy. It's My will for you.

Your loving Father

Knowledge

The Lord gives wisdom;
from his mouth come knowledge and understanding.
PROVERBS 2:6 RSV

The wise accumulate knowledge—a true treasure.
PROVERBS 10:14 MSG

Drinking from the beautiful chalice of knowledge
is better than adorning oneself with gold and rare gems.
PROVERBS 20:15 MSG

They won't go to school to learn about me,
or buy a book called God in Five Easy Lessons.
They'll all get to know me firsthand,
the little and the big, the small and the great.
HEBREWS 8:11 MSG

"If you'll hold on to me for dear life," says God,
"I'll get you out of any trouble.
I'll give you the best of care
if you'll only get to know and trust me."
PSALM 91:14 MSG

KNOW THY CHILD

"I dunno," she said as she blinked at her lie, refusing to rat on her brother.

"Yes, you do," her mom chided. "Now tell me who broke this lamp, or you'll be grounded."

You learn early in life that knowledge is power. At age ten, you would rather take the heat yourself than turn on your older brother. The knowledge of what really happened to mom's lamp translates into power in your relationship with both of them.

As you grow, you discover that some types of knowledge are more powerful than others. Knowing the daughter of your cheerleading coach is worth more in trade than knowing how to tuck in your sheets at the corners. Likewise, knowing how to style your hair in the latest trend carries greater influence than knowing your Aunt Martha's cookie recipe. The fact is, most people focus their energies on the types of knowledge that will win the advantage in society.

Now that you have a child, knowledge is more critical than ever—but not the knowledge of facts, dates, stats, trends, and fashion. The most crucial kind of knowing, other than the knowledge of God, is to know your child.

Make it your quest to discover his natural talents and her tender heart; explore his ability to reason and her passion for words. Ask nonthreatening questions that express deep interest. Listen carefully to explanations and dreams. Read your child like you would read a good book—making notes in the margins, underlining parts you need to commit to memory, and rereading the parts you don't understand.

Find adventure and discover delight in the journey into your child's heart, soul, and mind.

Love

This is how we know what real love is: Jesus gave his life for us.
So we should give our lives for our brothers and sisters.

1 John 3:16 NCV

Now that you have purified yourselves by obeying the truth
so that you have sincere love for your brothers,
love one another deeply, from the heart.

1 Peter 1:22

Love endures long and is patient and kind; love never is envious
nor boils over with jealousy, is not boastful or vainglorious,
does not display itself haughtily. It is not conceited (arrogant and
inflated with pride); it is not rude (unmannerly) and does not act
unbecomingly. Love (God's love in us) does not insist on its own
rights or its own way, for it is not self-seeking; it is not touchy or
fretful or resentful; it takes no account of the evil done to it
[it pays no attention to a suffered wrong]. It does not rejoice
at injustice and unrighteousness, but rejoices when right
and truth prevail. Love bears up under anything and
everything that comes, is ever ready to believe the best of every
person, its hopes are fadeless under all circumstances, and it
endures everything [without weakening]. Love never fails [never
fades out or becomes obsolete or comes to an end].

1 Corinthians 13:4-8 AMP

LOVE IS . . .

Being a mother requires love at the deepest level, and that love only grows stronger with each passing year. The Bible says:

According to 1 Corinthians 13:4-8, love is . . .
- patient—mild-tempered, composed, unruffled, imperturbable, tolerant, gentle, and calm.
- kind—tender, considerate, compassionate, benevolent, merciful, pleasant, sympathetic, understanding, and sweet.

Love is not . . .
- jealous—possessive, envious, resentful, demanding, monopolizing, mistrustful, suspicious, or insecure.
- boastful—bragging, pretentious, flaunting, or self-exalting.
- proud—arrogant, vain, insolent, cocky, snobbish, cavalier, overbearing, smug, aloof, stuck-up, or uppity.
- rude—impolite, ill-mannered, sullen, harsh, gruff, blunt, abrupt, tactless, curt, improper, insulting, or sarcastic.
- irritable—easily angered, touchy, ill-tempered, or moody.

Love does not . . .
- demand its own way—act in a self-seeking, greedy, miserly, insensitive, willful, stubborn, or obstinate manner.
- keep a record of wrongs—practice an unforgiving, resentful, or bitter disposition.
- delight in injustice—rejoice in disappointment or despair.

Love always . . .
- protects—guards, watches over, defends, secures, shelters, shields, cares for, harbors, and upholds.
- trusts—believes in, has confidence in, leans on, is convinced of, counts on, and has no reservations about.
- hopes—is expectant, looks on the bright side, is of good cheer, enthusiastic, emboldened, buoyant, and inspirited.
- perseveres—persists, stands firm by, continues, has stamina, is constant, is resolute, keeps on, and is tenacious.

Loyalty

What is desirable in a person is loyalty.

PROVERBS 19:22 NRSV

Many will say they are loyal friends,
but who can find one who is really faithful?

PROVERBS 20:6 NLT

If you love someone you will be loyal to him
no matter what the cost.

1 CORINTHIANS 13:7 TLB

The Lord is good. His love is forever,
and his loyalty goes on and on.

PSALM 100:5 NCV

Never let loyalty and kindness get away from you!
Wear them like a necklace; write them deep within your heart.
Then you will find favor with both God and people,
and you will gain a good reputation.

PROVERBS 3:3-4 NLT

With the loyal you show yourself loyal, [O Lord].

PSALM 18:25 NRSV

Heavenly Father:

One of Your most profound attributes is that You are loyal—You are faithful and true. You promise never to leave or forsake me, no matter what, regardless of the circumstances. I know how much that loyalty means to me, and I want to pass on that blessing to others, especially my children.

Father, it hurts me to watch those I love go through pain and loss. I want to do something to help. Often people need "Jesus with skin on" when they are going through tough times, and I offer myself to be used by You. Help me to be that loyal and dependable person, and show me how I can be the biggest blessing. Let those in need see You living through me, providing them the support and loyalty they need during such critical times.

Amen.

STANDING IN FOR MY BROTHER

He felt the sweltering heat as he opened the car door and stood aright. He had made the thirty-minute drive on this particular day for a reason.

Hard to believe three years have passed, he thought as he wove through the tombstones.

The grave marker was etched in his memory: "Face of an angel, heart of a warrior." It was larger than the infant buried there. He remembered the tiny casket and the anguish on his brother's face as he had carried it to its final resting place. He had felt his brother's pain. It had something to do with the way they grew up together. Living within the narrow walls of a small dwelling, their large family had always been close. No one cried without the whole family weeping. No one laughed without every voice chiming in.

Even after they all left home, Mom would call and say, "Your brother could use a friend." Nothing more. She simply kept them woven together as if the walls were still hugging them into each other's embrace.

Standing over his niece's grave, he realized he was the only living person there. *People don't visit cemeteries on August 9,* he figured.

But this was the day she had died and the day his brother had wept three years before . . . before the job forced him to move too far away to visit often.

So here I am, standing in his place because that is what brothers do.

"Where've you been?" his wife asked when he walked through the doorway later than usual.

"Standing in for my brother," he answered. "He'd have done it for me."

My Daughter,

I have empowered you to remain steadfast and loyal in the midst of difficulty. My strength will enable you to stand firm and strong for the people you love. As you are moved with compassion, follow your heart. What you feel is My love flowing through you. As you yield to Me, I will use you to wrap My arms around the brokenhearted.

Often during painful times, it seems as if many people become fair-weather friends, not wanting to become too involved, so it pleases Me that you want to "be there" for others in need. Your very presence will encourage them that I have not abandoned them, but rather that I remain as loyal and true as always. Reassure these hurting loved ones that better days are to come.

Your loving Father

Obedience

Children, obey your parents in the Lord, for this is right.
"Honor your father and mother"—this is the first commandment
with a promise: "so that it may be well with you and
you may live long on the earth." And, fathers, do not provoke
your children to anger, but bring them up in the discipline
and instruction of the Lord.

EPHESIANS 6:1-4 NRSV

What is more pleasing to the Lord: your burnt offerings and
sacrifices or your obedience to his voice? Obedience is far better
than sacrifice. Listening to him is much better than
offering the fat of rams.

1 SAMUEL 15:22 NLT

Jesus replied, "'Love the Lord your God with all your heart,
soul, and mind.' This is the first and greatest commandment.
The second most important is similar: 'Love your neighbor
as much as you love yourself.' All the other commandments
and all the demands of the prophets stem from these two laws
and are fulfilled if you obey them. Keep only these and
you will find that you are obeying all the others."

MATTHEW 22:37-40 TLB

Whenever you speak, or whatever you do,
remember that you will be judged by the law of love.

JAMES 2:12 NLT

KEEP IT SIMPLE

"Mom," the young woman said anxiously over the phone, "I'm worried about Abby. She's so disobedient."

"Honey, Abby's a good girl."

"No, Mom, she doesn't obey me. She's always getting into things and getting into trouble. She ransacks the DVDs, spills juice on the computer keyboard; she even breaks her own toys, on purpose, 'just as an experiment.' I don't remember us being that way, do you?"

"I suspect obedience was simpler back then," she said, letting her mind reach back in time.

"What do you mean simpler?" Kelly persisted.

"Back when you were small, there wasn't as much stuff, and there weren't so many choices."

"What's that got to do with anything?"

"The more stuff you have, the more rules you need to regulate the stuff."

"So you're saying that more rules mean more potential points of conflict; therefore, inevitably more conflict results?"

"Yes, that's right. But even more, children can get the impression that all the stuff is more important than they are. And that is when children get out of character."

"That sort of makes sense, but why does it work that way?"

"They get out of character when our values don't line up with God's value system. He values people first, not things. And since it is His image in which children are made, they have an internal instinct that challenges any system that perverts those values."

"So," Kelly said pensively, "the problem may be me—my values."

"Just think about it, honey. God has very few rules. In fact, one of them sums it all up: 'Treat people the way you want to be treated.' Obedience is about relationships, Kelly, not about rules."

Patience

We urge you, brethren, admonish the unruly,
encourage the fainthearted, help the weak,
be patient with everyone.
1 THESSALONIANS 5:14 NASB

Better is the end of a thing than its beginning;
and the patient in spirit is better than the proud in spirit.
ECCLESIASTES 7:8 RSV

We can rejoice, too, when we run into problems and trials
for we know that they are good for us—they help us learn
to be patient. And patience develops strength of character in us.
ROMANS 5:3-4 TLB

God will strengthen you with his own great power
so that you will not give up when troubles come,
but you will be patient.
COLOSSIANS 1:11 NCV

Always be humble, gentle, and patient,
accepting each other in love.
EPHESIANS 4:2 NCV

ATTITUDE DETERMINES OUTCOME

The incredible thing about attitude is that it determines behavior. For example, if you think you have the aptitude to learn something, you usually can. And amazingly, if you think you're patient, you probably are.

Patience as a disposition typically vacillates with the circumstances. You may start out being patient, but when the day gets long and people get annoying, you become impatient. That is, until you discover that you can harness your impulses and determine that you will be patient, in spite of everything going on around you.

Your toddler waddles in, pajama-clad, waking you early in the morning. "Mommy," his hoarse morning voice demands loudly, "I want waffles."

Your first impulse is to cover your head with the pillow and let out a muffled scream. "It's only six o'clock, for heaven's sake!"

But wait! Don't obey that first impulse; make your impulse obey you. Tell yourself that this miniature waffle-monger is a man in the making—an incredibly important, unbelievably heroic, astonishingly gifted man—who is requesting not just anyone's waffles . . . but your waffles! Then tell yourself that you are the most patient, responsive mother on the earth—none as long-suffering, unselfish, or attentive as you. Now, listen carefully as you hear yourself say, "I would love to make you waffles!"

Once the words fall from your lips, you become a firsthand witness to your own patient response. The rest is a downhill roll. You fall out of bed and in love with the day. You find yourself with reserves you knew not of. The more patience you practice, the more from whence to draw.

Sound silly, simplistic, and facetious? Don't knock it till you've tried it!

Peace

Let the peace of heart that comes from Christ be always present in your hearts and lives, for this is your responsibility and privilege as members of his body. And always be thankful.

COLOSSIANS 3:15 TLB

Jesus said, "I am leaving you with a gift—peace of mind and heart! And the peace I give isn't fragile like the peace the world gives. So don't be troubled or afraid."

JOHN 14:27 TLB

Following after the Holy Spirit leads to life and peace.

ROMANS 8:6 TLB

I will both lie down in peace, and sleep;
For You alone, O Lord, make me dwell in safety.

PSALM 4:8 NKJV

The Lord will give strength to His people;
The Lord will bless His people with peace.

PSALM 29:11 NKJV

Heavenly Father:

My life is so busy and my head becomes filled with all the things I need to accomplish throughout the day. I find my focus drifting from You to the details that one by one consume me. I may start the day in peace, but negative circumstances can develop quickly, and before I know it I'm filled with anxiety, worry, and stress.

I've gotten off track, Father. Help me to once again focus on You. Help me to keep my mind at peace as I move through my day knowing that You perfect all that concerns me. Help me to remember that my answers aren't found in analyzing my problems, but in conversing with You. Show me how to wait patiently as You work out the details. Teach me to rest in You—in a place of peace.

Amen.

PEACEFUL SURRENDER

"No God, no peace. Know God, know peace."

Have you seen that bumper sticker while sitting in five o'clock traffic while you're trying to get home in time to get dinner on the table for your family? You might have thought, *How in the world could knowing God bring me peace in the middle of rush hour?*

The secret is in surrender. Think of the slogan this way: Surrender to what you know about God and you will know peace.

What do you know about God?

- He is sovereign. God has absolute power.
- He is wise. God knows you better than you know yourself.
- He is attentive. God doesn't shrug you off.
- He is sensitive to your needs. God doesn't ignore or neglect you.
- He is mighty. God can do something about everything.
- He is open to your opinion. God esteems you so highly, He gave His Son for you.
- He is taking care of things you aren't aware of. God knows things you don't.
- He loves to converse with you about your concerns. God never tires of listening to you.
- He isn't troubled by your sleepless nights. God is up all night; He enjoys your company.
- He is trustworthy. God was doing this job long before you came along, and He can see it through.
- He is in control. God keeps the peace.
- He loves you. God never abandons, forsakes, or forgets you—even in five o'clock traffic.

As a mother, you set the emotional tone for your family. Knowing all that you know about God will enable you to fill your home with His peace, making it a safe haven from the storms of life.

My Daughter,

Great peace—the peace that passes understanding—is available to you. As My child, you
can walk through life composed and filled with
confidence in Me. As you surrender those things
you are worried about, you can rest, knowing that
I will take care of all that concerns you.

Come to Me and I will show you how to
handle every situation you face. That doesn't nec-
essarily mean it will always be easy, but you can
successfully maneuver through any storm if you'll
surrender to Me those things that threaten to
steal your peace.

I'm ready to lead you. Walk with Me and hold
My hand! Don't look to the right or left. Your
footsteps will be sure as you set your sights on
Me. I have already mapped your course through a
pathway of peace.

Your loving Father

Perseverance

Blessed is the man who perseveres under trial,
because when he has stood the test, he will receive the
crown of life that God has promised to those who love him.
JAMES 1:12

Pray at all times and on every occasion in the power
of the Holy Spirit. Stay alert and be persistent in your prayers
for all Christians everywhere.
EPHESIANS 6:18 NLT

May the Lord direct your hearts into God's love
and Christ's perseverance.
2 THESSALONIANS 3:5

In hope we have been saved, but hope that is seen is not hope;
for who hopes for what he already sees? But if we hope for
what we do not see, with perseverance we wait eagerly for it.
ROMANS 8:24-25 NASB

Be devoted to one another in brotherly love; give preference
to one another in honor; not lagging behind in diligence,
fervent in spirit, serving the Lord; rejoicing in hope,
persevering in tribulation, devoted to prayer.
ROMANS 12:10-12 NASB

A DIFFERENT PERSPECTIVE

There is a powerful secret in Scripture, couched within a peculiar set of circumstances, spoken by a man named Job. Let's listen in.

"Job," his wife sobbed, "we are ruined. Our children are dead, our livestock is gone, our servants have been murdered, and you are a walking corpse. We can't go on like this. Curse your God—the God who gave you great wealth and many children so that He could watch you writhe in anguish at the loss of them. Let's put an end to our lives and this agony."

"Dear wife, it is your grief that speaks such hopeless words. God is with us still," Job consoled.

"How can you say that? He mocks you!"

"No," Job assured her. "There is something in this that we cannot yet see. I trust that He will make it clear."

"Trusting Him makes you the fool," she cried.

"Though He slay me, yet will I hope in Him." Job stood his ground.

There it was—the secret to perseverance. It might be paraphrased: "Come what may, I trust in God." Job endured because he trusted that God had a perspective on the situation that he could not see. And Job was right! It was Satan, not the Lord, who had put him to the test. In time, everything was restored to Job—twice as much as before. He lived a long, joyful life because he persevered in hope. (See Job 2:1-10; 42:10-16.)

As a mother, you, too, will face many trials concerning your children, finances, and health. There is no greater testimony to the faithfulness of God than trusting Him in the face of all the heartache. Your perseverance will pay off.

Perspective

Great are the works of the Lord;
they are pondered by all who delight in them.

PSALM 111:2

You'll do best by filling your minds and meditating on things true,
noble, reputable, authentic, compelling, gracious—the best,
not the worst; the beautiful, not the ugly; things to praise,
not things to curse.

PHILIPPIANS 4:8 MSG

Be very careful never to forget what you have seen God doing
for you. May his miracles have a deep and permanent effect
upon your lives! Tell your children and your grandchildren
about the glorious miracles he did.

DEUTERONOMY 4:9 TLB

We couldn't be more sure of what we saw and heard—God's glory,
God's voice. The prophetic Word was confirmed to us.
You'll do well to keep focusing on it. It's the one light you have
in a dark time as you wait for daybreak and the rising of the
Morning Star in your hearts.

2 PETER 1:19 MSG

THE TREASURE CHEST
OF THE HEART

About the mother of Jesus, it was written, "Mary treasured up all these things and pondered them in her heart" (Luke 2:19).

What things? Those things that concerned her Son—the visit of some smelly shepherds claiming they had received an angelic birth announcement; the unsolicited testimony of a strange old man and strange old woman in the temple disclosing the true identity of her newborn child; the stellar compass—visible only to foreign dignitaries—signifying His succession to a throne; the astonishing experience of the youth lagging behind in Jerusalem to engage scholars in discussions of eternal weight; and even the voice of an angel stroking the early apprehension within her virgin soul.

Mary stored up these occurrences in her heart and meditated upon them frequently, striving to understand the Son she loved so deeply, longing to be the mother that the Father had commissioned her to be. It was a good thing, because the day was coming when a dark cloud of despair would gather to threaten her confident assumptions about Him—as it does for every mother at some point in her children's lives.

Fortunately, God has fashioned a mother's heart like a treasure chest where precious memories, insightful impressions, and cherished moments are tucked away. These critical reminders serve as witnesses to her children's worth—evidence upon which she can draw when a cloud of confusion or conflict hovers over her heart and mind.

Be a Mary-kind-of mother, preparing an inner treasure chest of hope. Then when the difficult times are upon you, draw out the treasure and refresh and renew yourself with its beauty.

Power

My speech and my preaching were not with persuasive words
of human wisdom, but in demonstration of the Spirit and
of power, that your faith should not be in the wisdom of men
but in the power of God.

1 CORINTHIANS 2:4-5 NKJV

We have this treasure in earthen vessels,
that the excellence of the power may be of God and not of us.

2 CORINTHIANS 4:7 NKJV

[The Lord] said to me, "My grace is sufficient for you,
for my power is made perfect in weakness." Therefore I will boast
all the more gladly about my weaknesses, so that Christ's power
may rest on me. That is why, for Christ's sake, I delight in
weaknesses, in insults, in hardships, in persecutions, in difficulties.
For when I am weak, then I am strong.

2 CORINTHIANS 12:9-10

Jesus said, "When the Holy Spirit comes to you,
you will receive power."

ACTS 1:8 NCV

You, dear friends, must build up your lives ever more strongly
upon the foundation of our holy faith, learning to pray in the
power and strength of the Holy Spirit.

JUDE 1:20 TLB

Heavenly Father:

What I need at this moment is Your mighty power. I've been far too dependent on my own strength, and as You knew would happen, my resources are spent. I'm worn out and discouraged.

Thank You for remaining faithful to me, even when I've failed to give You the proper place. My heart is overwhelmed, but I'm reaching for Your power. Infuse my spirit, soul, and body with the same resurrection power that raised Jesus from the dead. Heal my body and restore peace to my soul and spirit so that I can be strong in You once more.

Father, I don't want to fall into this trap again. Help me to recognize when I try to do things in my own power, and remind me that Your unlimited resources are available for the asking. Help me to set a good example for my children.

Amen.

WHO NEEDS TOUCHING?

"If I can just touch His clothes, I will be healed," the desperate woman whispered. She had heard about the Teacher—approachable and compassionate. It was rumored that He could work miracles. For twelve years, she had borne an infirmity for which no remedy had been found, though she had spent her life's savings searching for one.

But there was a problem. He was on His way to heal a dying child and was surrounded by people. Could she reach Him in time? Finally, at just the right moment, she seized the opportunity and touched His garment. She barely felt the fabric between her fingers before it slipped away, but it was enough. Suddenly she felt the weakness in her body turn to strength. She was healed.

Jesus realized that power had gone out from Him. "Who touched My clothes?" He asked, turning around.

"What do You mean, who touched You?" His friends asked. "It would be easier to determine who hasn't touched You."

But He persisted because Jesus felt His power—every nuance, every dimension, every effect of His power. (See Mark 5:25-34.)

As a mom, you have a unique influence in the life of your child. It is power of a human sort. But like the Lord's, it is an intuitive power. Something deep within a mother tells her when her strength is needed. She knows the power of her influence and when to use it. A godly mother feels her power, and in the integrity of her heart she wields it with the purest of motives.

When you sense your power has been tapped, or sense that someone needs the power of touch, take pause—as Jesus did—and answer the call.

My Daughter,

I desire to be your strength for every area of your life. I want to pour My power through you into the lives of your children and the other people you know. You don't have to wait until your heart is overwhelmed before you call on Me. I'm ready to intervene at the moment I hear your voice.

I have made an unlimited supply of My power available to you, whether you need it for strength, stamina, or physical healing. Anytime you feel powerless, come to Me and I will replenish you. I have all the strength you need and more. I will hold you up and help you accomplish whatever is necessary. Regardless of what you're facing, including giving strength to others, I have plenty of power to go around.

Your loving Father

Prayer

God's Decree— . . .
"They'll pray to me by name
and I'll answer them personally."
ZECHARIAH 13:8-9 MSG

Now this is the confidence that we have in Him,
that if we ask anything according to His will, He hears us.
And if we know that He hears us, whatever we ask, we know that
we have the petitions that we have asked of Him.
1 JOHN 5:14-15 NKJV

Jesus said, "Here's what I want you to do: Find a quiet,
secluded place so you won't be tempted to role-play before God.
Just be there as simply and honestly as you can manage.
The focus will shift from you to God, and you will begin to sense
his grace. The world is full of so-called prayer warriors who are
prayer-ignorant. They're full of formulas and programs and advice,
peddling techniques for getting what you want from God.
Don't fall for that nonsense. This is your Father you are dealing
with, and he knows better than you what you need.
With a God like this loving you, you can pray very simply."
MATTHEW 6:6-9 MSG

Why am I praying like this?
Because I know you will answer me, O God!
PSALM 17:6 TLB

ANGEL OR NO ANGEL

The angel Gabriel appeared to Zechariah while he was performing his priestly duty, saying, "Do not be afraid, Zechariah; your prayer has been heard" (Luke 1:13).

Zechariah was old, childless, and plagued with deep anxiety. He and his wife, Elizabeth, had long been beseeching God for a child of their own. And though devout, he now found himself on the threshold of giving up. It took an angel to convince him that his prayer had been heard and was being answered. As it turned out, his wife soon conceived a son—John the Baptist.

Every mother can identify with Zechariah's plight—the fear and anxiety that come from wondering if her prayer has been heard and answered. She begins praying during pregnancy for a healthy baby; throughout infancy and the toddler years, she asks for the development of the child's mind and body; then as adolescence rushes by, she prays for growth in character and signs of a healthy social life. By the time her son or daughter has secured a license to drive and some degree of freedom from her diligent watch, she finds herself praying for spiritual stamina and emotional safekeeping.

Thus, your faithful prayers ascend with those of devoted mothers everywhere as a constant hum in heavenly places. There are many voices, representative of one desire—petitioning the Almighty Abba for His blessing and favor. Never lose heart, never cease to hope, never give in to the fear that God does not hear, and always believe that your prayers have been answered—angel or no angel.

Priorities

If you really fulfill the royal law according to the Scripture, "You shall love your neighbor as yourself," you do well.

JAMES 2:8 NKJV

People were bringing little children to Jesus to have him touch them, but the disciples rebuked them. When Jesus saw this, he was indignant. He said to them, "Let the little children come to me, and do not hinder them, for the kingdom of God belongs to such as these." . . . And he took the children in his arms, put his hands on them and blessed them.

MARK 10:13-14,16

Jesus said, "The King will say . . . , 'Come, you who are blessed by my Father, inherit the Kingdom. . . . For I was hungry, and you fed me. I was thirsty, and you gave me a drink. I was a stranger, and you invited me into your home. I was naked, and you gave me clothing. I was sick, and you cared for me. I was in prison, and you visited me.' "Then these righteous ones will reply, 'Lord, when did we ever see you hungry and feed you? Or thirsty and give you something to drink? Or a stranger and show you hospitality? Or naked and give you clothing? When did we ever see you sick or in prison, and visit you?' And the King will tell them, 'I assure you, when you did it to one of the least of these my brothers and sisters, you were doing it to me!'"

MATTHEW 25:34-40 NLT

IRRITATING INTERRUPTIONS OR DIVINE APPOINTMENTS?

Teaching children how to determine priorities requires time and patience, but like most adults, you probably still struggle with this yourself. One very effective approach by Stephen Covey in his best-selling book, *The Seven Habits of Highly Effective People*, is beginning by identifying your various roles in life. You then move to determine goals within those roles and list activities which lead toward the realization of those goals. Finally, you put those activities into priority order. The success of this approach lies in the intentional steps taken every day toward a variety of objectives.

There is, however, one critical component that is not addressed in the book. It is the priority of interruptions.

When you read about the life of Christ—the most influential man who ever lived—you are struck by the fact that His life was a series of interruptions from people demanding His attention and assistance. With less than three years to accomplish a mission so vast—it spanned the whole of human history and penetrated eternity with overwhelming victory—He did it through a series of divinely appointed interruptions designed to impact the hearts of people with the love of God . . . one touch at a time.

While teaching your children how to deal with priorities—and continuing your own education—be sure to include the importance of being responsive to people's needs . . . those potentially irritating interruptions, which hold forth the promise of genuine blessing. These divine appointments need no prioritizing, for they are already the highest priority of the Holy One.

Purity

God, examine me and know my heart; . . .
See if there is any bad thing in me.
Lead me on the road to everlasting life.

PSALM 139:23-24 NCV

Happy are those who live pure lives,
who follow the Lord's teachings.

PSALM 119:1 NCV

Jesus said,
"Blessed are the pure in heart,
for they will see God."

MATTHEW 5:8

Who may ascend into the hill of the Lord?
Or who may stand in His holy place?
He who has clean hands and a pure heart.

PSALM 24:3-4 NKJV

Confess your faults one to another,
and pray one for another, that ye may be healed.

JAMES 5:16 KJV

Heavenly Father:

When my children look at my life, I want it to reflect an image of You. Create in me a clean heart, sifting and exposing the impurities so that I can confront them. Help me not to justify them, but to be quick to remove them from my heart and life.

As I remove old habits that resist my Christian lifestyle, help me to incorporate new habits that are pleasing to You. When I slip, I know that You forgive me as soon as I ask, but help me to forgive myself.

Make me a vessel of honor, pure and holy before You. Help me to demonstrate a life of purity before my children. I give myself to You and commit to changes that are necessary to live my life in a way that is more pleasing to You.

Amen.

CONFESSION: A FILTER
FOR THE HEART

"What's a nice girl like you doing in a place like this?" is a familiar question. A similar question might be, "How's a mom like you going to teach children like yours to live right in a world gone wrong?"

Here's one suggestion: teach your children purity of heart by practicing confession. Naturally, you stress the importance of having pure motives and keeping a pure heart. But every human being is prone to error. The impact that confession has upon an impure heart can be very beneficial to growth in purity. It makes a lot of sense if you look at it from a practical point of view.

When a landowner digs a new well for drinking purposes, he sends a water sample to the lab to test for impurities. If the water tests clean, he installs a pump and voila! Bottoms up!

However, if the water tests impure, the proprietor installs a special water filter that is designed to siphon off the chemicals and bacteria that can cause disease. The purified water is then safe for consumption.

Confession is like a water filter, which separates the pure from the impure elements. Those impurities, which get caught in the sieve of honest self-evaluation, are the things that need to be taken to God in prayer and extracted from the heart. The amazing thing is that once an impurity is exposed by confession, it is easier to detect the next time it attempts to infiltrate the heart.

Teach your children to maintain purity of heart; but teach them also how to effectively deal with the impurities of the heart, which show up in spite of their best efforts.

My Daughter,

In order to grow, you must change. As you read My Word, you will find that certain passages penetrate your heart more forcefully than others. That is one of the ways that I speak to you about the adjustments you need to make. As impurities are exposed, don't feel condemned, over-whelmed, or afraid of the challenge to change. I love you and am here to help.

With each day, your desire to reflect My image will cause My character and nature to grow inside of you. The more of Me that you take in— through My Word or by yielding to the Holy Spirit—the more your own selfish desires will be pushed out.

Change is good! And as your children witness your growth in Me, they will be inspired to grow too.

Your loving Father

Purpose

Whatever you do, work at it with all your heart,
as working for the Lord, not for men.

COLOSSIANS 3:23

Jesus said, "Now My soul has become troubled; and what shall I say,
'Father, save Me from this hour'? But for this purpose I came to
this hour. Father, glorify Your name."

JOHN 12:27-28 NASB

The apostle Paul said, "David, after he had served the purpose
of God in his own generation, fell asleep, and
was laid among his fathers."

ACTS 13:36 NASB

We know that God causes all things to work together for good
to those who love God, to those who are called
according to His purpose.

ROMANS 8:28 NASB

Be sure that you live in a way that brings honor to the Good News
of Christ. Then . . . I will hear that you are standing strong
with one purpose, that you work together as one
for the faith of the Good News.

PHILIPPIANS 1:27 NCV

The Son of God came for this purpose: to destroy the devil's work.

1 JOHN 3:8 NCV

"YOU DID THAT ON PURPOSE!"

Purpose as a philosophy is getting a lot of good press these days. People are reading and talking about realizing and fulfilling a higher purpose in life. Yet recalling earlier days, you can probably remember when the word *purpose* was more commonly used as an indictment against you, an accusation of wrongdoing. "You did that on purpose!" Susie said, pointing an accusing finger. Or, "Mom, she hit me on purpose," Jimmy whined, hoping that the consequence would mean sentencing to the furthest extent of the law . . . your mom's, that is.

Stated either way—negatively or positively—the idea of purpose implies intention. What your purpose is, or what you do on purpose, both indicate intentional living. The ultimate goal in life, according to the Scriptures, is to glorify God. In the way you live among your family; in your employment; in the way you treat people in public, in traffic, or in line at the grocery store—you are to reflect the glory of the Lord intentionally.

Some people can identify a specific role to which they feel called, while others cannot. Some recognize a vision they must pursue; others answer the call to follow a visionary. In all, the purpose—which is to glorify God—custom-fits every life for the accomplishment of the one goal.

So whatever you do, do it on purpose. Do it to glorify the Lord. Your intentional good will speak volumes to your children in seeking their purpose in life.

Rejection

Even if my father and mother abandon me,
the Lord will hold me close.
PSALM 27:10 NLT

Praise be to God,
who has not rejected my prayer
or withheld his love from me!
PSALM 66:20

The Lord will not reject his people;
he will never forsake his inheritance.
PSALM 94:14

The Lord says,
"I took you from the ends of the earth, . . .
I have chosen you and have not rejected you."
ISAIAH 41:9

Jesus said, "Go at once into the streets and alleys of the town, and
bring in the poor, the crippled, the blind, and the lame."
LUKE 14:21 NCV

EYES OF COMPASSION

"His disciples asked Him, 'Rabbi, who sinned, this man or his parents, that he was born blind?'

"'Neither this man nor his parents sinned,' said Jesus, 'but this happened so that the work of God might be displayed in his life'" (John 9:2-3).

Everyone in the area knew the man. Born blind, he was an outcast due to the assumption that his condition was the result of a shortfall. Because he had suddenly received his sight, the religious leaders—those who had judged him unworthy—were up in arms. Summoning him to the chambers of the high council, they demanded to know how he had been healed.

Knowing their judgment of him and others like him, he said, "There is a man named Jesus who is teaching a new message. He cares about people like me and insists He is only mirroring God's concern for people. He did this."

"Who do you think you are?" they sneered. "Presuming you are something in God's eyes."

Rejection has little to do with the condition of the person being rebuffed; it is more a reflection of the dark heart of him who casts others aside.

So what are we to do when a child suffers the pain of rejection? Teach him or her what Jesus taught this blind man about spiritual blindness.

"I have come into this world, so that the blind will see and those who see will become blind" (v. 39).

The trouble isn't with those who are rejected; it is that the one who rejects others is blind to the truth about the worth of all people. Have pity on the shortsighted, for they cannot see God; and always have eyes of compassion for those whom the world rejects.

Relationships

By yourself you're unprotected.
With a friend you can face the worst.
ECCLESIASTES 4:12 MSG

"Imagine a person who lives well, treating others fairly,
keeping good relationships— . . .
This person who lives upright and well
shall live a full and true life."
EZEKIEL 18:5,9 MSG

It's better to have a partner than go it alone.
Share the work, share the wealth.
And if one falls down, the other helps.
ECCLESIASTES 4:9-10 MSG

Jesus said, "Here is a simple, rule-of-thumb guide for behavior:
Ask yourself what you want people to do for you,
then grab the initiative and do it for them."
MATTHEW 7:12 MSG

Laugh with your happy friends when they're happy; share tears
when they're down. Get along with each other; don't be stuck-up.
Make friends with nobodies; don't be the great somebody.
ROMANS 12:15-16 MSG

Heavenly Father:

Help me to understand the true importance of relationships. You know it's not always easy for me to nurture them. It takes so much effort to reach out and be friendly.

As I work on this area of my life, remind me that it's not about what I have to say. Help me listen to others and glean wisdom from them that will enrich my life. When I'm tempted to throw up walls when others reach out to me, make me aware of it and help me to be receptive.

Relationships are obviously very important to You since You sent Your Son to redeem all people everywhere. Help me to see others the way You do, and show me what I have to offer. Bring the people into my life to whom I can be a blessing and who will enrich me and help me grow in You.

Amen.

RELATIONSHIPS RULE!

Whether you are helping your child to develop relationships or working on your own, the following suggestions are proven methods for deepening your intimate connection with others:

1. Treat your friend as if he or she means more to you than anything. Devote some uninterrupted time and attention to the relationship on a regular basis. Be focused, never allowing petty distractions to tempt your eyes and ears away from the conversation in which you are engaged. Listen with genuine interest and respond with intelligent questions or comments.

2. Be open and honest. Develop the art of authenticity and mutual vulnerability. One sure way to let someone know you care is to let them into the chambers of your heart. If your friend senses that your guard is up, theirs will go up too.

3. Be expressive. Let love find a voice. There's no need to be gushy; just put words and skin on your emotions so your friend will have evidence of your affection.

4. Recognize the rites of friendship. Special times, special places, and special gifts create a unique kind of connection. Be thoughtful and creative in your friendship rituals.

5. Let go, for love's sake. Don't suffocate your friend by demanding control. Relax your expectations and your demands upon the relationship and it will flourish in the freedom.

6. Laugh hard, cry hard, play hard, and pray hard. Be intense and intentional with your sense of humor, your compassion, your energy, and your faith.

Relationships nurtured in this manner will last longer than a lifetime—they'll soar right into eternity!

My Daughter,

I do place great value on relationships. I gave My own Son so I could restore the relationship between myself and the wonderful people I created. I want to know them—and you—intimately, and I want you to know Me.

Every person is a treasure chest of gifts waiting to be opened by others. Friendship offers an opportunity to tap into those treasures and experience the uniqueness that I've placed in each individual.

Iron sharpens iron. As you exchange life with those special people whom I place in your life, you each help the other to grow and become more of whom I created you to be. Be bold and courageous. Step up and be friendly as I bring people into your life. Something exciting is sure to happen.

Your loving Father

Repentance

I am happy, not because you were made sorry, but because
your sorrow led you to repentance. For you became sorrowful
as God intended. . . . Godly sorrow brings repentance that leads to
salvation and leaves no regret, but worldly sorrow brings death.

2 CORINTHIANS 7:9-10

This is what the Lord says:
"If you repent, I will restore you
that you may serve me."

JEREMIAH 15:19

Do you despise the riches of His goodness, forbearance,
and longsuffering, not knowing that the goodness of God
leads you to repentance?

ROMANS 2:4 NKJV

Jesus said, "With my authority, take this message of repentance
to all the nations, beginning in Jerusalem: 'There is forgiveness
of sins for all who turn to me.'"

LUKE 24:47 NLT

The Lord God, the Holy One of Israel, has said,
"In repentance and rest you will be saved."

ISAIAH 30:15 NASB

TRUTH APPLIED WITH THE SALVE OF GRACE

A genuine change in behavior can be a very long and arduous process for a child. After all, it takes time to develop a habit of misbehavior to begin with, so it will likely take time to unravel. Undesirable behavior usually begins with small steps in the wrong direction, picking up momentum when positive reinforcement comes in the form of social acceptance, self-gratification, of a cover-up for lack of performance.

Communication is vital to the process. Talking about what is wrong is only one side of the issue, and unfortunately it is where many parents end the conversation. Discussing why it felt right to do something wrong is the other side, and it is just as critical. Children need to know that their parents can help them deal with the motivation for doing wrong, not just with the wrong itself.

The real difficulty lies in helping the child understand why the behavior is unacceptable. Recognizing your disapproval is one thing, but coming to a conviction of why his or her own behavior is unacceptable is another. This is why the process of repentance can be slow-going. Children usually feel resentment before they experience repentance, particularly when there is any form of discipline involved.

The Scriptures say that Jesus came to restore fellowship between God and His wayward children. He accomplished the task, but repentance from their hearts was a vital part of the mission. That which was most critical in bringing about the necessary repentance was the two-pronged characteristic of grace and truth—the truth about God's love applied with irre-sistible grace.

Truth and grace are still the only effective means by which children are brought to repentance.

Respect

Let the wife see that she respects and reverences her husband
[that she notices him, regards him, honors him, prefers him,
venerates, and esteems him; and that she defers to him, praises
him, and loves and admires him exceedingly].

EPHESIANS 5:33 AMP

Pay to all what is due them— . . . respect to whom respect is due,
honor to whom honor is due.

ROMANS 13:7 NRSV

We appeal to you, brothers and sisters, to respect those who labor
among you, and have charge of you in the Lord and admonish you;
esteem them very highly in love because of their work.
Be at peace among yourselves.

1 THESSALONIANS 5:12-13 NRSV

Never speak sharply to an older man, but plead with him
respectfully just as though he were your own father. Talk to the
younger men as you would to much-loved brothers. Treat the older
women as mothers, and the girls as your sisters, thinking
only pure thoughts about them.

1 TIMOTHY 5:1-2 TLB

Since we respect our fathers here on earth, . . . should we not all the
more cheerfully submit to God's training so that we can begin
really to live?

HEBREWS 12:9 TLB

STANDING ON TIPTOE

"Aaron, respect shouldn't be something that folks must earn," his mother challenged. "Respect is something you give freely because you have it within you."

"I can't respect him, Mom. What he did was wrong."

"Have you forgotten that at times you have fallen short too?"

"No," Aaron answered, "but I've never falsified information in order to gain an advantage."

"Are you sure?" She turned to stir the soup.

"What's that supposed to mean?" Aaron felt an arrow of insult in her question.

"Once when you were young, you told me that Mitch had eaten his candy bar so I gave you his. Mitch was a little upset when it turned out you ate both of them."

"Mom! I can't believe you would bring up something so trivial!"

"The point is, it didn't shake our confidence in you," she said as she glanced over her shoulder to gather his expression. "We still treated you like the Aaron you had always been, and we were right to do so."

"Well, the stakes are a little higher in this situation. This isn't just about a candy bar."

"Still, it is about the same issue—integrity," his mother countered. Aaron realized that she had a point. "You're right to hold him accountable," she continued as she turned to face him again, "but do it by holding him to a higher standard. It'll help him believe in himself—to know that he is capable of being who you thought he was.

"Remember how we used to measure you boys by making a mark on the door?" she asked. "You always craned your neck, trying to reach your brother's mark. Funny thing about respect," she smiled. "Folks will usually stand on tiptoe trying to measure up to the mark you've made for them."

Restoration

My friends, if anyone is detected in a transgression,
you who have received the Spirit should restore such a one in a spirit
of gentleness. Take care that you yourselves are not tempted.
Bear one another's burdens, and in this way
you will fulfill the law of Christ.

GALATIANS 6:1-2 NRSV

Since we were restored to friendship with God by the death
of his Son while we were still his enemies, we will certainly
be delivered from eternal punishment by his life.

ROMANS 5:10 NLT

My brothers and sisters, if one of you wanders away from the truth,
and someone helps that person come back, remember this: Anyone
who brings a sinner back from the wrong way will save that sinner's
soul from death and will cause many sins to be forgiven.

JAMES 5:19-20 NCV

In his kindness God called you to his eternal glory by means of
Jesus Christ. After you have suffered a little while, he will restore,
support, and strengthen you, and he will place you on
a firm foundation.

1 PETER 5:10 NLT

Heavenly Father:

When I discipline my children, they often
resist and resent me. It's hard for me to correct
them—it takes so much energy! It would be easier
to turn a blind eye, but I would be shirking my
responsibility to train them.

First, help me to exercise self-control, so I
won't react in anger. Then give me the strength
to confront their wrong actions. Move on their
hearts to admit their wrongs and to take responsibility for them. Then give them the grace to
repent, to turn and go in the other direction.

After they have done their part, help me to
forgive my children the way that You do, to drop
the matter once and for all. Then restore us all to
a right relationship with You and each other.
Knit our hearts together with Your love.

Amen.

THE SOFTENING OF
HARD HEARTS

The parched earth bakes dry in the August heat—so dry that it loses its resilience and the surface cracks, taut from want of moisture. The ground, thirsting for relief, becomes hard and resistant to the rain. When it does finally begin to drizzle, the precipitation cannot penetrate at first. Yet eventually, when steady and persistent, the moisture lubricates the crusty sod; and before you know it, it is drinking with a craving that cannot be quenched.

People's hearts are like the sun-baked earth when, through long spells of spiritual drought, they become hardened and unyielding. But like the rain, the mercy of God falls persistently into their lives—soaking into their conscience and softening them up until finally they find themselves gulping at His grace with deep appreciation. That is the meaning of restoration.

When you or your children experience the heartache of someone's wrongdoing, there must eventually come a time of restoration. Not a partial, half-hearted sprinkling of reparation; but a drenching, cleansing, healing downpour of revival. That is the nature of grace. It gives people a brand-new beginning. There's no probationary period demanding proof of performance; no holding out, holding back, or holding down like shackles chained to one's ankles.

Restoration provides the freedom to get past the hurt and get on with living! It is the celebration that comes when what was lost has been found. It is the compassion of honest souls breathing life back into the fallen.

Teach your children to cherish the idea of restoration—both given and received—by living it and by giving it.

My Daughter,

When a piece of furniture is restored, it is brought back to its original—and often better—condition. The same is true in restoring people. Jesus' death and resurrection restored the gap between the entire human race and Me. Now we can have an even better relationship than I experienced with Adam and Eve before the Fall, because now I live in My children! In addition, when people are born again, they become far better than they were before. They become entirely new creatures in Christ!

I am all about restoration, between people and Me and between people amongst themselves. Teach these things to your children, and never allow pride or your desire to avoid conflict keep you from seeking restoration with them. Rely on My strength to forgive and bring a new beginning to all of your relationships.

Your loving Father

Reward

Whoever would draw near to God must believe that he exists and
that he rewards those who seek him.

HEBREWS 11:6 RSV

Jesus said, "Love your enemies. Pray for those who hurt you.
If you do this, you will be true children of your Father in heaven.
He causes the sun to rise on good people and on evil people,
and he sends rain to those who do right and to those who do wrong.
If you love only the people who love you, you will get no reward."

MATTHEW 5:44-46 NCV

Jesus said, "When you do good things, don't do them in front of
people to be seen by them. If you do that, you will have no reward
from your Father in heaven. . . . Your giving should be done
in secret. Your Father can see what is done in secret,
and he will reward you."

MATTHEW 6:1,4 NCV

By faith Moses, when he was grown up, refused to be called the son
of Pharaoh's daughter, choosing rather to share ill-treatment with
the people of God than to enjoy the fleeting pleasures of sin.
He considered abuse suffered for the Christ greater wealth
than the treasures of Egypt, for he looked to the reward.

HEBREWS 11:24-26 RSV

PEOPLE ARE THE PRIZE

It's a frustrating thing about most rewards: you don't get them until the end, after all the excitement is over, and they are very short-lived. For instance, your reward at the end of a footrace is a ribbon. The reward for studying hard in school is a well-marked report card. The reward for winning the state championship is a trophy for your school.

But, you might argue, the merits of racing include building endurance and greater physical strength. A good student will land a better job and advance more quickly. And the state champion may move on to the NFL or the NBA.

That is correct; however, the rewards for those advanced accomplishments are still temporal and have very little impact upon eternity.

But there is good news! In the book of Ephesians, the apostle Paul wrote that the reward for being faithful to God and to people is having eternal relationships with both!

That makes sense when you consider that relationships are the only thing on the earth that will survive into eternity. Wealth, position, power, fame, material possessions—none of those things will transfer into eternal realms.

Because the reward is people, it follows that people should be your highest priority. From those who occupy your household to strangers in the street, your reward will be multitudinous.

If you find yourself striving after rewards related to success, accomplishments, wealth, or any other thing, your children will probably follow suit. If, however, your children sense that you value others as your ultimate inheritance, your reward will come as they become heroes, humanitarians, and the champions of noble causes.

Righteousness

I consider everything a loss compared to the surpassing greatness of
knowing Christ Jesus my Lord, for whose sake I have lost all things.
I consider them rubbish, that I may gain Christ and be found in
him, not having a righteousness of my own that comes from the law,
but that which is through faith in Christ—the righteousness
that comes from God and is by faith.

PHILIPPIANS 3:8-9

God made him who had no sin to be sin for us,
so that in him we might become the righteousness of God.

2 CORINTHIANS 5:21

[The Lord] blesses the home of the righteous.

PROVERBS 3:33

The mouth of the righteous is a fountain of life.

PROVERBS 10:11

The tongue of the righteous is choice silver, . . .
The lips of the righteous nourish many. . . .
The mouth of the righteous brings forth wisdom. . . .
The lips of the righteous know what is fitting.

PROVERBS 10:20-21,31-32

THE RIGHT BRAND

Righteousness. It sounds like a sticky, religious word. It carries the reputation of being stiff and starchy, not warm, fleshy, and real. But what a shame, for the word *righteousness* actually means "to be rightly related." Being rightly related to God means understanding that He is sovereign and you are not. In other words, it means living your life respecting His sovereignty and being aware of your frailty.

The phrase "Righteous, Dude!"—made popular by post-hippie-wanna-bes—probably falls more in line with the real meaning of righteousness than all the pious-sounding expostulations of self-righteous people.

Here's a short list of what it should conjure up in your mind.

Righteousness should have a ring of authenticity—a genuine concern for the welfare of others.

Righteousness should hold forth the grace of a merciful God in the face of scandalous failure.

Righteousness ought to spring like a life-giving fountain from the grateful hearts of those rescued from their fall.

Righteousness should walk softly among those who've been shattered along with their dreams.

Righteousness ought to mend the broken shards of hearts rent by betrayal.

Righteousness should not boast of perfect performance, but sing of perfect love.

Righteousness, if understood aright and correctly applied, should bring great relief to people suffering from the loneliness of self-appointed exile.

By establishing your family as a righteous one—one where each member is rightly related to God and to each other—you will ensure that when your children hear the word *righteousness,* they'll know it is the right brand.

Sacrifice

I will not sacrifice to the Lord my God burnt offerings
that cost me nothing.
2 SAMUEL 24:24

May he remember all your offerings
and accept all your sacrifices.
PSALM 20:3 NCV

The sacrifice God wants is a broken spirit.
God, you will not reject a heart that is broken and sorry for sin.
PSALM 51:17 NCV

We know love by this, that he laid down his life for us—
and we ought to lay down our lives for one another. How does
God's love abide in anyone who has the world's goods and sees a
brother or sister in need and yet refuses help?
1 JOHN 3:16-17 NRSV

Put your trust in the Lord, and offer him pleasing sacrifices.
PSALM 4:5 TLB

Brothers and sisters, since God has shown us great mercy,
I beg you to offer your lives as a living sacrifice to him.
ROMANS 12:1 NCV

Heavenly Father:

Many times I sacrifice my time, energy, and resources so that I can give to my children. I didn't buy that dress and those shoes I wanted so that my boys could go to baseball camp. I went without a car so that my teenage daughter could drive mine. I realize, however, that any sacrifice I make is nothing compared to the sacrifice You made by offering Jesus as the ransom for us.

In turn, Father, I offer my life as a sacrifice for You. Show me how I can do that in practical ways every day. Show me where I can make the best use of the gifts and talents You've placed inside me. I offer them to bless my family and all the people You bring my way.

Amen.

MORE THAN MERE PENNIES

"Mama," the young man frowned, "you're looking thinner every day."

"Plenty to eat, and food to spare," she said. It wasn't a lie. She did have all she wanted. But she was tired these days, and her interest had turned to the needs of others more important to her.

"Do you have money?"

"I have plenty, and some to spare." That wasn't untrue, either. She was painfully aware of her son's growing family; she couldn't complain about her own situation in light of their increasing needs. She had enough.

"I trust that you will tell me when you run out . . . of food . . . or money," he hugged her into his chest. "Yes, Mama?"

"Yes, my son," she kissed his neck. "I'm off to the temple now," she said, pinching the two copper coins tightly between her fingers. These were her last, and he must not know.

Jesus sat opposite the place where the offerings were given and watched the old woman approach the treasury box. He read her lips as she prayed, "Thank You, Lord, for Your bountiful blessings."

He said to His friends, "This poor widow has put in more than all the others" (Luke 21:3).

"What do You mean, Lord?" Peter asked. "She gave less than a penny."

Jesus replied, "All these people gave their gifts out of their wealth; but she out of her poverty put in all she had to live on" (v. 4).

As a mother, you sacrifice constantly—your time, your energy, your own desires. While your children may not realize the extent of your sacrifice until they have children of their own, you can bet that your heavenly Father knows, and He says, "Well done."

My Daughter,

Many people think that throwing money into the offering plate is sacrifice—and for many it is. But sacrifice means full surrender. When you obey with a willing heart, placing your desire to please Me above your desire to hold on to what you have, that's sacrifice. It reflects that You trust Me on a deep level.

Don't compare what you give with what others do. Sacrifice looks different from person to person. When you give what you value or cherish most—when you give your very best—that is true sacrifice. When you give your time for others, when you could be doing something for yourself, that's sacrifice.

Trust Me to know what you can do for My kingdom and for others. Give with an open hand.

Your loving Father

Sensitivity

Be gentle with one another, sensitive.

EPHESIANS 4:32 MSG

When you sit down to a meal, your primary concern should not be
to feed your own face but to share the life of Jesus. So be sensitive
and courteous to the others who are eating. Don't eat or say or do
things that might interfere with the free exchange of love.

ROMANS 14:21 MSG

Isn't it wonderful all the ways in which this distress has goaded
you closer to God? You're more alive, more concerned,
more sensitive, more reverent, more human, more passionate,
more responsible. Looked at from any angle, you've come out of
this with purity of heart.

2 CORINTHIANS 7:11 MSG

We were as gentle among you as a mother feeding and
caring for her own children.

1 THESSALONIANS 2:7 TLB

As the elect of God, holy and beloved, put on tender mercies,
kindness, humility, meekness, longsuffering.

COLOSSIANS 3:12 NKJV

GOD'S REIGN . . . GREAT JOY

In a section of Scripture known as the Beatitudes (see Matthew 5:3-12), Jesus profiles the person in whom God's reign has been firmly established. Here it is, modified to fit motherhood:

The mother who recognizes that she is spiritually helpless—at the end of her rope—will find great joy in discovering that God has shown deep sensitivity to her need for mercy and grace.

The mom who grieves over her own failings will find great joy in the understanding and compassion that God extends to her.

The mother who is likewise sensitive to the failings of her children and gentle in dealing with them will find great joy in helping them overcome.

The mom who finds herself desiring more of God's goodness and less of self will find great joy and contentment in her life—lavishing His goodness and grace upon her household.

The mother who is sensitive to her children's needs and merciful in dealing with them finds great joy in God's sensitivity to her needs.

The mom who has deep integrity toward her children will find great joy in her own relationship with her Heavenly Father.

The mother who brings peace to her surroundings and seeks peace between loved ones will find great joy in the peace of mind that God gives His loved ones.

The mom whose commitment to God and family is misunderstood and ridiculed by outsiders will find great joy in God's sensitivity to her need for His approval and reassurance.

In summary, the mother whose heart is attuned to God will find great blessing in sharing her joy in Him with her children.

Service

Jesus said, "Your attitude must be like my own, for I,
the Messiah, did not come to be served, but to serve, and
to give my life as a ransom for many."

MATTHEW 20:28 TLB

Jesus said, "The one who serves you best will be your leader.
Out in the world the master sits at the table and is served by
his servants. But not here! For I am your servant."

LUKE 22:26-27 TLB

Never be lazy in your work but serve the Lord enthusiastically.

ROMANS 12:11 TLB

Jesus said, "Whoever wishes to become great among you
shall be your servant."

MATTHEW 20:26 NASB

Serve the Lord with gladness!

PSALM 100:2 RSV

Train yourself to serve God. Training your body helps you
in some ways, but serving God helps you in every way by bringing
you blessings in this life and in the future life, too.

1 TIMOTHY 4:7-8 NCV

THE HIGHEST CALLING

The time had come. He must leave His friends and return to His Father. Knowing they would suffer heartache and loss over Him, He was sad to go. But He knew that they would find great consolation and joy in serving others just as He had in serving them. There's something uniquely gratifying in giving your life away.

This would be His last meal with them. They had shared so many meals together—resting after a day's activities, swapping stories, laughing, discussing deep spiritual truths, and rejoicing in their friendship. His eyes must have misted over as He realized that this was to be the last.

When the moment was right, He rose from the table. Moving toward the wash basin, He removed His outer garment and wrapped a large towel around His waist. Looking more like a slave than a teacher, He poured water into the large bowl and returned to the table, kneeling down beside His disciples. He removed the worn sandals and began washing the dusty, tired feet of His dear friends. It shocked them all. For a moment, they were speechless.

Finally, refusing to allow the Master to do servants' work, Peter exclaimed, "You shouldn't be washing our feet!"

"If I don't, you can't be My partner," Jesus replied.

"What are You doing?" Peter asked.

"Then let Me teach you that which brings Me the greatest joy."

As Jesus finished washing the feet of His stunned disciples, He proceeded to explain. "Since I, the Lord and Teacher, have washed your feet, you ought to wash each other's feet. I have given you an example to follow: do as I have done to you. . . . That is the path of blessing" (John 13:14-15,17 TLB).

This is what motherhood is all about.

Sincerity

Who may worship in your sanctuary, Lord? . . .
Those who lead blameless lives
and do what is right,
speaking the truth from sincere hearts.

PSALM 15:1-2 NLT

Now that you have purified your souls by your obedience to the
truth so that you have genuine mutual love, love one another deeply
from the heart. . . . Rid yourselves, therefore, of all malice,
and all guile, insincerity, envy, and all slander.

1 PETER 1:22; 2:1 NRSV

Let us come near to God with a sincere heart and a sure faith,
because we have been made free from a guilty conscience,
and our bodies have been washed with pure water.

HEBREWS 10:22 NCV

In everything we have done in the world, and especially with you,
we have had an honest and sincere heart from God. We did this by
God's grace, not by the kind of wisdom the world has.

2 CORINTHIANS 1:12 NCV

May God's grace and blessing be upon all who
sincerely love our Lord Jesus Christ.

EPHESIANS 6:24 TLB

Heavenly Father:

Forgive me for putting my reputation before my children. I know it's wrong to care what others think of me at the expense of my relationships at home. Help me to be sensitive to my children's needs and feelings, and give me the courage to overcome my pride so that I can give them the priority treatment they deserve.

I want to show my children the same sincere and unconditional love that You've shown me. I want them to feel cherished and loved—because they are! Help me to think of words that will motivate, inspire, and encourage their young hearts. As their biggest fan, I want to hear them say, "Mom, you really made me believe in myself!"

When I'm tempted to be insincere, tap me on the shoulder and remind me that I get only one chance to be the best mother I can be!

Amen.

FOR SOMEONE ELSE'S SAKE

"Six days of the week have been set aside for healing!" he shouted in anger. The religious leaders were up in arms about the violation of the Sabbath, and as the synagogue ruler, his spotless reputation was now smeared. "Come on those days if you want to be made well." Never mind that he'd just witnessed a miracle; he had a good mind to expel the woman who had caused him this embarrassment. She'd been eighteen years in her arthritic condition. What would one more day have mattered?

"You hypocrites!" Jesus interrupted, exposing the real motives behind the ruler's words. Jesus knew that the ruler only gave the appearance of caring about God's people and their needs, when in reality, this leader was using the position for his own benefit.

"Doesn't each of you on the Sabbath untie his ox or donkey from the stall and lead it out to give it water?" Jesus continued, pointing out that the religious leaders obviously cared more for their animals than for God's children. "Then should not this woman, a daughter of Abraham, whom Satan has kept bound for eighteen long years, be set free on the Sabbath day from what bound her?" (Luke 13:15-16).

This humiliated all of Jesus' opponents, but the people were delighted by the freedom that His teaching proclaimed.

Be certain that your motive toward your children is genuine. If your concern for your reputation is more important than your child's needs or feelings, they will know.

My Daughter,

What good does it do for you to teach a Bible study, lead prayer, and mentor women in your church if your own children don't know Me personally? Or what if they resent Me because you spend more time at the church than with them?

The gifts I have placed within you are for specific seasons in life. Your family's health—physically as well as spiritually—is your first priority now. It is sad, but repeatedly men and women speak from the platform to thousands in the congregation, while their own children are turned off to the truth of My Word because they missed out on the unconditional love and concern of their parents.

Give your attention to your children today. You have only a short time to invest in them. Make sure they know that your heart is passionate toward them.

Your loving Father

Spiritual Growth

Like newborn babes, long for the pure spiritual milk,
that by it you may grow up to salvation.

1 PETER 2:2 RSV

Speaking the truth in love, we are to grow up in every way
into him who is the head, into Christ.

EPHESIANS 4:15 RSV

We are bound to give thanks to God always for you . . .
because your faith is growing abundantly, and the love of every one
of you for one another is increasing.

2 THESSALONIANS 1:3 RSV

When you proclaim his truth in everyday speech,
you're letting others in on the truth so that they can grow and
be strong and experience his presence with you.

1 CORINTHIANS 14:3 MSG

We are joined together in his body by his strong sinews, and we grow
only as we get our nourishment and strength from God.

COLOSSIANS 2:19 NLT

Grow in the grace and knowledge of
our Lord and Savior Jesus Christ.

2 PETER 3:18 RSV

A JOURNEY OF FAITH

Peter, a wise old diplomat with a deep love for God's people, wrote the following words of advice to a group of struggling believers (paraphrased from 2 Peter 1:3-9):

The more you know Jesus, the more you'll experience His power. You'll find out for yourself that He wants to share the good life and His glory with you! His mighty power stands behind His amazing promises, including the promise that you can escape the wrongdoing in the world and become more like Him. So lay claim to His promises, and thereby grow spiritually.

You can begin by having the faith to say no to temptation. If you do, the Lord will give you the strength to follow through on your word. This step of moral excellence taken in good faith will actually make you feel closer to God than you have in the past and inspire the desire and confidence to spend more time with Him, to get to know Him better.

The more time you spend with Him, the more you'll want to be like Him—a most effective motivation for practicing self-control. Self-control is like boot camp for the soul, training you for endurance, stamina, and greater resilience. You will learn to trust Him more.

All of these things add up to godly character; and in godly character you will find the strength to express love for all people.

Spiritual growth is a journey upon which you and your children may embark together. As you trust God in daily matters, walking down the path mapped out above, together you will reach the point of maturity. Then you can be effectively involved in the lives of others.

Strength

I pray that from his glorious, unlimited resources he will give you
mighty inner strength through his Holy Spirit.

EPHESIANS 3:16 NLT

May our Lord Jesus Christ and God our Father, who loved us
and in his special favor gave us everlasting comfort and good hope,
comfort your hearts and give you strength in
every good thing you do and say.

2 THESSALONIANS 2:16-17 NLT

Those who hope in the Lord
will renew their strength.
They will soar on wings like eagles;
they will run and not grow weary,
they will walk and not be faint.

ISAIAH 40:31

A wife of noble character who can find? . . .
She sets about her work vigorously;
her arms are strong for her tasks. . . .
She is clothed with strength and dignity.

PROVERBS 31:10,17,25

HAIRY SCARE!

"Mommy, look at me! I'm strong!"

Samson must have said those words to his mother when he was small. Do you remember his story? An angel announced to his mother that she would give birth to him and placed special stipulations on her during pregnancy. He was dedicated to the Lord from birth and was forbidden to cut his hair or drink a glass of wine. He was a long-haired teetotaler with the body of Arnold Schwarzenegger and had a weakness for women. And most significantly, he was strong.

The trouble with strength is that it makes you vulnerable. If you are weak, people don't care . . . they simply aren't interested. But if you have a unique strength of character, talent, physique, or ability, you can count on someone trying to exploit you, manipulate you, or simply want your attention and affection.

Samson was vulnerable to the beautiful Delilah. She always wanted him to reveal the secret of his strength, and he willingly played along, making up riddles in response. In the end, however, she wore him down and betrayed him to his enemies who lopped off his curly locks. This violation of God's directives caused the Lord to depart from Samson, who then became as weak as any man. His life ended tragically—blind and in captivity. (See Judges 13:1-7,24; 16:1-30.)

Who knows? Maybe Samson's mom tried to teach him about being vulnerable to women. It is a wise mother who teaches her children—male or female—to guard their strength by keeping their relationship with the Lord in good repair. Somehow there was a connection between Samson's physical strength and his long hair, but his real strength was in his relationship with God.

Thankfulness

In everything give thanks;
for this is the will of God in Christ Jesus for you.
1 THESSALONIANS 5:18 NKJV

By Him let us continually offer the sacrifice of praise to God,
that is, the fruit of our lips, giving thanks to His name.
HEBREWS 13:15 NKJV

The Lord is my strength and my shield;
my heart trusts in him, and I am helped.
My heart leaps for joy
and I will give thanks to him in song.
PSALM 28:7

I will give you thanks in the great assembly;
among throngs of people I will praise you.
PSALM 35:18

It is good to give thanks to the Lord,
And to sing praises to Your name, O Most High;
To declare Your lovingkindness in the morning,
And Your faithfulness every night.
PSALM 92:1-2 NKJV

Heavenly Father:

Forgive me for not taking the time to thank You for all that You are in my life. I am truly thankful, but I don't say it nearly enough. I don't mean to take You for granted, but sometimes I do.

I want to have a thankful heart that takes notice of even the smallest things You so generously give me. I don't want to miss any of the blessings that You provide. Thank You for the air I breathe, the home I live in, the people in my life. Thank You for my children and the difference their presence makes every day.

Instill in me a grateful heart and show me how to express my thanks for all the little things that mean so much to me. Most of all, I'm thrilled to have a friend like You.

Amen.

BIG THANKS FOR SMALL FAVORS

"Thank you," the woman said, following him to the van. "Thank you so much!"

"Sure," Steve said. He had just gotten his permit and had hoped he could drive home from the store, but now it just seemed too trifling to bring up.

"What was that about?" his mom asked, once the door was shut.

"It was no big deal."

"You must have done something to invoke that kind of response," she said.

"It was just a little bitty thing. I was waiting in line to pay for the milk and this little kid walked up to the candy rack and just stared at it with tears in his eyes."

"What happened?"

"His mom walked up with a couple more kids and I could see that they were really, really poor. All of a sudden his mom whispers, 'Honey, you know I would buy you a candy bar if I had the money.'"

"Then what?" his mom was tearing up too.

"I slipped a ten-dollar bill into the little guy's pocket and said, 'Hey, dude, get everyone in the family a candy bar, okay?'"

"No wonder his mom felt such gratitude!"

"Really, it was nothing, Mom."

"To you, maybe . . . " she smiled. "But to me, you're a champion! By the way, you want to drive home?"

"Oh, thank you," he said. "Thank you so much!"

A great big thank you for a little bitty thing goes a long, long way in the heart.

My Daughter,

Thankfulness is one of My favorite gifts to receive. It offers Me time with you to hear what means the most to you. When you brag on the magnificence of a sunset or the splendor of a mountain view, I learn that you appreciate My artistry and the beauty I created for you.

When you express your thankful heart, you let Me know just how much your relationship with Me means to you. When you sing praises to My name, it opens the door to a deeper relationship between us where we can freely exchange our love.

Thanksgiving testifies to My goodness and reminds Me of all the promises I've made to you. I hear you and say, "Hey, My daughter is blessing My holy name!"

Your loving Father

Thoughts

We demolish arguments and every pretension that sets itself up
against the knowledge of God, and we take captive every
thought to make it obedient to Christ.

2 CORINTHIANS 10:5

The word of God is living and active, sharper than
any two-edged sword, piercing to the division of soul and spirit,
of joints and marrow, and discerning the thoughts
and intentions of the heart.

HEBREWS 4:12 RSV

Be careful what you think,
because your thoughts run your life.

PROVERBS 4:23 NCV

Fix your thoughts on what is true and honorable and right.
Think about things that are pure and lovely and admirable.
Think about things that are excellent and worthy of praise.

PHILIPPIANS 4:8 NLT

As he thinks in his heart, so is he.

PROVERBS 23:7 NKJV

CAPTIVE THOUGHTS

In so many words, Jesus once said, "You are what you think about." In fact, He took it a step further; He said that what consumes one's conversation reveals what occupies one's heart.

Does that last statement find you scrambling to remember your last several conversations, asking yourself, *What have I been harping on? What have I unintentionally disclosed?* It could be anything from the latest diet trend to the death of your pet parakeet. Whatever it is, it strikes at the heart of what you are on the inside.

Suddenly you realize that if that is true for you, it is true for everyone else too. Now your mind hurries to the conversations you've recently had with others, analyzing their words and dissecting their deepest thoughts.

One psychologist suggested that if you were to videotape yourself for a couple of weeks, you would likely be astonished at how you appear from the outside looking in. In fact, you would probably feel betrayed by your own behavior! Your body language, words, facial expressions, gestures, and interactions with others all combine to reveal your thoughts from the deepest chambers of your heart.

Here is an interesting point to consider: Your children have an instinctive understanding concerning what Jesus said. Children have the uncanny ability to perceive people correctly. Whether it is because they are unencumbered or perhaps uninhibited, they intuit the truth about adults with amazing accuracy. Try as you will, you cannot fake your way; your words will eventually betray you!

In light of these facts, you might want to give some thought to what you're thinking about. The apostle Paul advised that you should take every thought captive to God's way of thinking.

Time

See then that you walk circumspectly, not as fools but as wise,
redeeming the time, because the days are evil.

EPHESIANS 5:15-16 NKJV

To every thing there is a season,
and a time to every purpose under the heaven.

ECCLESIASTES 3:1 KJV

It is time to seek the Lord,
that he may come and rain righteousness upon you.

HOSEA 10:12 NRSV

Lord, remind me how brief my time on earth will be.
Remind me that my days are numbered,
and that my life is fleeing away.

PSALM 39:4 NLT

O my people, trust in him at all times.
Pour out your heart to him,
for God is our refuge.

PSALM 62:8 NLT

TIME: SPEND SOME, INVEST SOME, AND SAVE SOME

One young mother E-mailed her mom:

"Where have the past three years gone? Today, Jesse and I purchased his nap mat and backpack for preschool. He was so excited that he spent the rest of the day packing and unpacking his things. I, on the other hand, spent the day secretly crying over the end of an era, now forever in the past."

Her mother wrote back: "One day, when you were about eight years old, I was marveling at how much you had grown, and I suddenly realized that somewhere in time past I had lifted you from the floor and into my arms for the last time. Somehow, without my knowing, you had outgrown it. Tears sprang into my eyes for I had committed that unthinkable last rite of mothering without knowing it! I felt robbed! Why didn't someone notify me that it was to be the last time I would do that? I would have lingered there, savoring every moment of that embrace until . . . until . . . until . . .

"It was then that I realized why a mother must not know, for if she did, the child would never escape the custody of her relentless love."

How can a mother redeem the time she has with her children? Not by grieving over time past, time lost, or time squandered, but by making the most of the time at hand.

Time is a precious commodity. Spend some in playful endeavor, invest some in quiet conversation, and save some by making good memories!

As Benjamin Franklin stated, "Dost thou love life? Then do not squander time, for that is the stuff life is made of."

Trials

In this you greatly rejoice, even though now for a little while, if necessary, you have been distressed by various trials, so that the proof of your faith, being more precious than gold which is perishable, even though tested by fire, may be found to result in praise and glory and honor at the revelation of Jesus Christ.

1 PETER 1:6-7 NASB

No test or temptation that comes your way is beyond the course of what others have had to face. All you need to remember is that God will never let you down; he'll never let you be pushed past your limit; he'll always be there to help you come through it.

1 CORINTHIANS 10:13 MSG

The Lord knows how to rescue godly men from trials.

2 PETER 2:9

Dear friends, don't be surprised at the fiery trials you are going through, as if something strange were happening to you. Instead, be very glad—because these trials will make you partners with Christ in his suffering, and afterward you will have the wonderful joy of sharing his glory when it is displayed to all the world.

1 PETER 4:12-13 NLT

We can rejoice, too, when we run into problems and trials, for we know that they are good for us—they help us learn to endure.

ROMANS 5:3 NLT

Heavenly Father:

I've become tired and disappointed in the midst of the difficult circumstances in my life. My patience is exhausted; and I'm tempted to be angry with You, others, and myself. I want to give up!

Help me to persevere through this trial, Father. I want to hang on, but I feel myself slipping. Waiting and keeping my eyes on You is so hard. My mind wanders, replaying imagined outcomes. I know You have the answers, and I need to rest in Your peace.

Help me to find motivation to press past my discouragement. Give me the words to say to my children in the midst of this trial. Reveal the wise answers that they will be able to understand.

You have promised that Your grace is sufficient, so I hope in Your Word.

Amen.

PHANTOMS IN THE STORM

"Why didn't He come with us?" James shouted as he clutched the mast. The storm was worsening.

"After feeding all those people, He just wanted to be alone," John answered loudly into the wind.

It was sometime between three and six o'clock in the morning. Jesus had spent the night praying in the hills after sending the people home and His disciples across the lake. He was aware of the storm and had His eye on their progress. He was also aware that another storm was brewing, but of a spiritual sort.

The squall blew out of nowhere. Relentlessly, the wind battered the boat while the waves swelled into angry walls of resistance, refusing them the shore. Though seasoned sailors, the disciples grew edgy and apprehensive as exhaustion began to take its toll.

Suddenly, in the eerie darkness, fear struck, causing the threat of the storm to pale in comparison. Jesus came walking across the restless sea to show them that His sovereignty reached beyond the merely physical realm.

"A-a-a-a-a-agh!" Andrew screamed at the sight of the phantom-like figure riding the swells, His garment whipping fiercely in the wind.

On the other side of the boat, Thomas jerked his head in the direction of Andrew's terrified gaze. "He-e-e-e-elp!" he yelled. "It's a ghost!"

"Take courage! It is I. Don't be afraid," Jesus shouted (Matthew 14:27).

Often the most trying—even frightening—circumstances hold forth the most brilliant opportunity to encounter the Lord. Be prepared; you might meet up with Him where you least expect Him.

My Daughter,

Jesus said, "These things I have spoken to you, that in Me you may have peace. In the world you will have tribulation; but be of good cheer; I have overcome the world" (John 16:33 NKJV). It's true—I have given you all that you need to move through this valley. When you find your journey hard, look to Me for encouragement. Hope in Me and find strength in My Word.

It is persevering through trials and difficulties that makes you stronger. Only in the midst of opposition can you discover the glory of My strength being perfected in your weakness.

I've known your end from the very beginning, and I have great plans for you. Never give up on your dream. I love you with an everlasting love. Together we will push through to the next mountaintop!

Your loving Father

Trust

The king trusts in the Lord;
through the unfailing love of the Most High
he will not be shaken.

PSALM 21:7

In you our ancestors trusted;
they trusted, and you delivered them.
To you they cried, and were saved;
in you they trusted, and were not put to shame.

PSALM 22:4-5 NRSV

Those who know the Lord trust him,
because he will not leave those who come to him.

PSALM 9:10 NCV

My enemy will say, "I have overcome him,"
and my foes will rejoice when I fall.
But I trust in your unfailing love;
my heart rejoices in your salvation.

PSALM 13:4-5

BEGIN WHERE YOU ARE

Watching an accomplished ballerina onstage, the little girl longed to imitate the graceful movements she admired.

"Mama, I'm going to dance like that when I get home."

Little does she suspect that beneath the glamorous skirt and tights, there are well-developed muscles, strong and practiced for performance, which took years of diligence and training.

"Mama, why can't I dance like that ballerina?" she whines later at her failed attempt.

"You can," her mother consoles. "But you will have to begin where you are, practicing little steps every day, and after some time, you'll be able to dance like that."

Likewise, having observed a home-run hitter in a professional baseball game, one little boy yearned for sports stardom.

"Mom, I'm going to hit like that when I get home."

He stands before his makeshift home plate with feet placed perfectly, knees bent just so, bat held high, and swings! He misses.

"Mom, why can't I hit like that professional baseball player?"

"You can," his mother consoles. "But you'll have to begin where you are, practicing little swings every day, and after some time, you'll be able to hit like that."

A young mother watches an old woman suffer courageously through the death of her husband after sixty years of marriage, while bravely consoling her children in their loss.

"Lord, I want to trust like that when I get old."

Yet the young mother cries at trifling matters, sobbing over a dented bumper.

"Lord, why can't I trust like that old, grieving woman?"

"You can," He consoles. "But you'll have to begin where you are, practicing in little ways every day, and after some time, you'll be able to trust like that."

Truth

We will not hide these truths from our children but
will tell the next generation about the glorious deeds of the Lord.
We will tell of his power and the mighty miracles he did.

PSALM 78:4 NLT

Truth stands the test of time; lies are soon exposed.

PROVERBS 12:19 NLT

Our responsibility is never to oppose the truth,
but to stand for the truth at all times.

2 CORINTHIANS 13:8 NLT

The Lord's promise is sure. He speaks no careless word;
all he says is purest truth, like silver seven times refined.

PSALM 12:6 TLB

Cross-examine me, O Lord, and see that this is so;
test my motives and affections too. For I have taken
your lovingkindness and your truth as my ideals.

PSALM 26:2-3 TLB

A wise person is hungry for truth, while the fool feeds on trash.

PROVERBS 15:14 NLT

AMEN, AMEN!

In ancient Israel, before the time of Christ, some of the prophets used the phrase, "Thus saith the Lord." What they meant was that the words they were about to speak were not spoken on their own initiative, but were words spoken on the authority of God. They were announcing, "The words I am about to speak are words of absolute truth."

It was in this context, for example, that the prophet Amos said, "Seek the Lord and live" (Amos 5:6).

When Jesus came teaching, He employed the use of a unique phrase, as well: "I tell you the truth." These words indicated that He was going to lay something profound upon the hearts of His hearers. In the original language of the New Testament scriptures the term was "Amen, amen," which is Greek for "It is true, it is true." These words implied a greater authority than the words the prophets had used because Jesus was not merely speaking the truth—He was the truth. Jesus was the truth, while the prophets had been only the voice of truth. And the reason for His saying it twice was to indicate that the matter was firmly established by God the Father and reinforced by God the Son.

It was in this context that Jesus said, "I tell you the truth, my Father will give you whatever you ask in my name" (John 16:23).

When teaching your children about truth, seek the source of truth—Jesus, who is full of grace and truth. Jesus—the way, the truth, and the life. Then you will know the truth, and the truth will set you free.

Understanding

Make me understand what you want;
for then I shall see your miracles.

PSALM 119:27 TLB

How great he is! His power is absolute!
His understanding is unlimited.

PSALM 147:5 TLB

I have more understanding than the elders,
for I obey your precepts. . . .
I gain understanding from your precepts;
therefore I hate every wrong path.

PSALM 119:100,104

I pray also that you will have greater understanding in your heart
so you will know the hope to which he has called us and that
you will know how rich and glorious are the blessings
God has promised his holy people.

EPHESIANS 1:18 NCV

The fear of the Lord is the beginning of wisdom;
a good understanding have all those who practice it.
His praise endures for ever!

PSALM 111:10 RSV

Heavenly Father:

Sometimes I forget to look at life from my children's perspective. The things that seem insignificant to me can be enormously important to them; likewise, what's important to me may seem trivial to them. We need Your help to understand each other.

Help me to look deeper than my children's questions of "Why?" Give me insight into what they are thinking and what is prompting their questions; then help me to answer them on a level they can identify with.

I also need Your help to know what makes my children tick so I can be the best mother I can be. You created them, so You know exactly what will bring out the best in them. I want to understand my children just as You do.

Amen.

OUTSTANDING IN THEIR FIELD

When training for a customer-service position, you might encounter a crash course in psychology that addresses an interesting phenomenon known as the field of emotion. In a nutshell, you learn that in order to be effective in handling complaints, you must learn to mirror your customer's emotion. In other words, you enter their field of emotion. It makes your customer feel understood and that helps establish trust.

The good news is, it works! And if you become proficient, people might say, "She's outstanding in her field"—her field of emotion, that is.

But did you know that this technique came right out of the Bible? Jesus used this strategy in dealing with people, not because it was an effective technique, but because He felt genuine compassion for people. When His dear friends Mary and Martha grieved the death of their brother, Jesus wept. Certainly He knew what He was going to do. He was going to shout into that smelly tomb, "Lazarus, come out!" And though the man had been dead four days, he would rise up, reclaim his spirit, and leap out of his grave clothes. Nevertheless, Jesus cried with His friends.

If this is the way Jesus dealt with people, why wouldn't this work with your children? Instead of scolding them for being angry, immediately affirm their anger. Then once they feel understood, move to dealing rationally with the upset. Or disappointment, or fear, or sorrow, or frustration. The refreshing thing about children is that they exist in a different field of emotion every few minutes. Why not be "out standing" in their field . . . yes, out standing right by their side!

My Daughter,

Rest assured that you have all that is necessary for you to be the mother your children need. I chose you to parent them because I knew you could prepare them better than anyone else for all that I've called them to do. I've placed an understanding within you to know and discern their hearts.

Take a little extra time and observe them, much like you did when they were newborns. Ask the Holy Spirit, your teacher, to help you see the little things in your children that will help you gain understanding into how they think, what is important to them, and how they perceive the world.

Above all, realize that you have what it takes. The answers they—and you—need will always be found in Me.

Your loving Father

Unity

Conduct yourselves in a manner worthy of the gospel of Christ, so
that . . . I will hear of you that you are standing firm in one spirit,
with one mind striving together for the faith of the gospel.

PHILIPPIANS 1:27 NASB

Jesus . . . looked up to heaven and said, "Father . . . I have given
them the glory you gave me—the glorious unity of being one,
as we are—I in them and you in me, all being perfected into one—
so that the world will know you sent me and will understand
that you love them as much as you love me."

JOHN 17:1,22-23 TLB

Make every effort to keep the unity of the Spirit
through the bond of peace.

EPHESIANS 4:3

May the God who gives endurance and encouragement give
you a spirit of unity among yourselves as you follow Christ Jesus,
so that with one heart and mouth you may glorify the God
and Father of our Lord Jesus Christ.

ROMANS 15:5-6

Complete my joy by being of the same mind, having the same love,
being in full accord and of one mind.

PHILIPPIANS 2:2 RSV

FORTIFYING THE FAMILY

The ancient city of Ephesus in Asia Minor was a thriving seaport and the most important trade center of its day. It was also the center of a deeply-rooted heathen religion founded upon gross sensuality. Those who held to faith in God were in a vast minority, while posing a real threat to those whose livelihood depended upon the idolatrous practices of that religion. Opposition to Christianity intensified and the family of God realized the critical need for unity as a means of survival.

Paul wrote a letter to those believers who addressed unity as an essential method of fortifying their faith in the face of adversarial relations. Ironically, he claims that unity is found in self-denial rather than self-assertion. Here are the key ingredients:

- Humility . . . the selflessness that doesn't need to be noticed, but regards other people with genuine esteem.
- Gentleness . . . the gracious and tender consideration of another point of view or another person's needs.
- Patience . . . the perseverance and resilience on another person's behalf, compelled by genuine love.
- Peace . . . the eternal bond that Christ created with His costly grace.

According to Paul, unity will come about only when there is a common commitment to these four characteristics within the heart of every participant.

Perhaps you feel that things haven't significantly changed since the days of Ephesus. You may feel that the culture in which you are rearing your children is driven more by economics and sensuality than by godliness and principle. If so, concentrate your efforts at home on building unity with which to fortify your family's faith for the future.

Unselfishness

Jealousy and selfishness are not God's kind of wisdom.
Such things are earthly, unspiritual, inspired by the devil.

JAMES 3:15 TLB

Those who belong to Christ Jesus have crucified their own sinful
selves. They have given up their old selfish feelings and
the evil things they wanted to do.

GALATIANS 5:24 NCV

Jesus said to the disciples, "If any of you wants to be my follower,
you must put aside your selfish ambition, shoulder your cross,
and follow me."

MATTHEW 16:24 NLT

Let all men know and perceive and recognize your unselfishness
(your considerateness, your forbearing spirit).

PHILIPPIANS 4:5 AMP

Do nothing from selfishness or conceit,
but in humility count others better than yourselves.

PHILIPPIANS 2:3 RSV

SHARE, AND BE SHARED!

At the heart of unselfishness is the willingness to share—your time, talents, material goods, space, energy, wisdom, affection, ideas, etc. Sharing these aspects of your life builds trust and intimacy with another person. But perhaps the greatest test of unselfishness is the willingness to share the individual with whom you share.

In every meaningful relationship there is some degree of ownership wherein the individuals involved lay claim to each other. For instance, parents and children feel a mutual sense of entitlement to each other in comparison to what outsiders feel. This possessiveness, whether minimal or intense, exists in marriage, friendship, and even relationships at school, church, or at work. It is a natural part of living and it leaves people with a healthy sense of belonging.

However, when one party becomes possessive in a selfish way, the relationship becomes unhealthy and unproductive. Selfishness can do its greatest damage in this context, destroying precious ties among families and friends.

How can you promote an unselfish standard within your home?

1. Respect the uniqueness of each individual in your family.
2. Respect the opinions of others.
3. Respect the needs of others.
4. Finally, respect the relationships of others. No one is the all-sufficient one in relationship to another. People need a variety of friendships to reside in the many different chambers of their hearts.

Be unselfish with the people you love. They'll love you for sharing!

Values

If anyone is causing divisions among you, he . . .
has a wrong sense of values.

TITUS 3:10-11 TLB

Jesus said, "Either make the tree good, and its fruit good;
or make the tree bad, and its fruit bad; for the tree is known by its
fruit. . . . For out of the abundance of the heart the mouth speaks.
The good person brings good things out of a good treasure, and the
evil person brings evil things out of an evil treasure."

MATTHEW 12:33-35 NRSV

A wife of noble character is her husband's crown.

PROVERBS 12:4

Jesus said, "My Father is glorified by this,
that you bear much fruit and become my disciples."

JOHN 15:8 NRSV

Jesus said, "You did not choose Me, but I chose you and
appointed you that you should go and bear fruit, and that your fruit
should remain, that whatever you ask the Father in My name
He may give you."

JOHN 15:16 NKJV

Heavenly Father:

I want to look like You. I want others to see You in me. Help me to choose what You esteem as valuable over my own selfish desires.

There are so many times when my emotions get the best of me—especially in front of my children. Help me to cultivate the fruit of Your Spirit—joy, peace, patience, kindness, goodness, faithfulness, gentleness, and self-control. And above all, help me to choose love at every opportunity. If I can walk in love first, it will cause my actions and words to conform to the image You have of me—the image I want my children to have of me.

I want these things to be so fully developed in me that they overflow and impact for good all the people You've placed in my world.

Amen.

PEACHY PRINCIPLES

If you long to know what God values, take a look at Jesus; He was a walking, talking, interactive visual aid for God's value system. The defining principles of His life are known as the fruit of the Spirit. In fact, Jesus used a wonderfully vivid metaphor when in John 15:5, He said, "I am the vine; you are the branches." He continued by explaining that the branches yield fruit consistent with the vine upon which they grow. It makes so much sense.

The fruit of the Spirit Jesus referenced in His metaphor happens to be a savory cluster of character traits that contribute wholeness to relationships and promote purpose in living. They are love, joy, peace, patience, kindness, goodness, faithfulness, gentleness, and self-control.

Imagine if those enticing attributes were to dangle in lush clusters from the hearts of people you encounter every day. These values have the capacity to effect a radical change in society that could rock the world with peace and goodwill.

The interesting thing about these values is that they come packaged as a unit. You can't pick and choose the traits that come easiest for you, excluding those that you find difficult. In fact, they are interdependent. Where one exists, the other is starting to bud. If one starts to rot, the rot infects the whole bushel. And they all spring from the primary fruit of love.

They say the apple doesn't fall far from the tree. If you want your children to live according to God's values, you will have to be their visual aid—loving well, deeply, expressively, unconditionally, and forever.

My Daughter,

I have asked you to bear much fruit, fruit that reflects My love for you. A seed cannot produce after its own kind unless it first falls to the ground and dies. Likewise, you have been crucified with Christ. Your old, fallen nature is dead, and you have been raised to new life in Christ. Now You have My character as part of your nature. As you give place to it, this fruit can grow and flourish.

I am love. When you choose to love—you choose to put Me first in all that you do. That brings honor to My name and draws others to Me through you. Thank you for your willingness to serve Me by choosing to bear fruit. Embracing what I value allows you to become successful in every good work.

Your loving Father

Victory

Victory comes from you, O Lord.
May your blessings rest on your people.

PSALM 3:8 NLT

Hear the shouts, hear the triumph songs
in the camp of the saved?
"The hand of God has turned the tide!
The hand of God is raised in victory!"

PSALM 118:15-16 MSG

Do your best, prepare for the worst—
then trust God to bring victory.

PROVERBS 21:31 MSG

God also says:
"When the time's ripe, I answer you.
When victory's due, I help you."

ISAIAH 49:8 MSG

In the Messiah, in Christ,
God leads us from place to place
in one perpetual victory parade.

2 CORINTHIANS 2:14 MSG

A WIN FOR ALL

The boys had been training for weeks. Jett had the build of a runner, but Trey was older and faster.

The night before the race, Jett lay on his bed frowning.

"What's up, little brother?" Trey asked.

"I'm just thinking about tomorrow."

"You nervous?" the older sibling teased.

"I just know I can't win," Jett mumbled. "I don't know why I'm running."

"Jett, at your age, you don't enter the race only on the chance you can win," he replied. "When I was your age, I wasn't winning."

"But you didn't have a brother competing against you."

"An older brother," Trey reasoned. "Dude, I'm proud of you. You're the youngest one in the race."

"You may be proud, but Mom is going to be embarrassed."

"You're crazy, Jett, Get some sleep."

The next morning in the starting block, Trey sensed his younger brother's anxiety. *Jett is going to have to deal with it; I've got to stay focused*, he reasoned.

Midway down the track Trey moved out in front of the runners. Just as he entered the straightaway, Trey heard one of the runners tumble head over heels to the ground, letting go a familiar cry. Without hesitation, he darted off to the side of the track, forfeiting his lead, falling to his knees beside Jett.

"What are you doing, stupid," Jett scowled. "You were winning."

"There's no victory in crossing the finish line first if my brother is out of the race," he smiled.

Far from embarrassing her, a mother's goal is realized when the love of one child champions another!

Vision

This is God's Word on the subject:
" . . . I know what I'm doing. I have it all planned out—
plans to take care of you, not abandon you,
plans to give you the future you hope for."
JEREMIAH 29:10-11 MSG

The Lord . . . said:
"Write the vision
And make it plain on tablets,
That he may run who reads it.
For the vision is yet for an appointed time;
But at the end it will speak, and it will not lie.
Though it tarries, wait for it;
Because it will surely come,
It will not tarry."
HABAKKUK 2:2-3 NKJV

As it is written:
"Eye has not seen, nor ear heard,
Nor have entered into the heart of man
The things which God has prepared for those who love Him."
But God has revealed them to us through His Spirit.
1 CORINTHIANS 2:9-10 NKJV

ENVISIONING THE END RESULT

There is a peculiar visual impairment known in laymen's terms as tunnel vision. Those plagued with this disorder lose their peripheral sight. It is actually a type of blindness, for though there is sight, it is so severely restricted that it distorts one's reality.

Tunnel vision is a rare medical condition, yet unfortunately, not so rare when it comes to parents having a vision for their children. Many parents suffer from tunnel vision. Arriving at some noble goal for their child, a mother can lose sight of any vision that the child might develop independent of her.

For example, seventeen-year-old Greg loves animals and cherishes the dream of becoming a veterinarian. His mother, on the other hand, thinks that engineering is much more suitable. Greg makes a visit to Auburn University with several other applicants, bent on examining their pre-vet program. Upon his return home, his mother inquires about the school of engineering.

"They do it all, Mom: electrical, mechanical, industrial, you name it. But that isn't what I researched."

"What did you spend your time doing, for heaven's sake?"

"I visited with some science professors, checked out their labs, and got to shadow a vet intern. It was great!"

"I can't believe you wasted your time and my money on that nonsense," she exclaims.

Greg slinks to his room, certain that his mother's vision is more about herself than about him.

As a mom, be sure you have a clear vision for your children—a vision so broad and resilient that it can encompass all of the aspirations they have for themselves.

Wisdom

Fools think their own way is right,
but the wise listen to advice.
PROVERBS 12:15 NRSV

Wisdom will make your life pleasant
and will bring you peace.
As a tree produces fruit, wisdom gives life to those who use it,
and everyone who uses it will be happy.
PROVERBS 3:17-18 NCV

There's nothing better than being wise. . . .
Wisdom puts light in the eyes,
And gives gentleness to words and manners.
ECCLESIASTES 8:1 MSG

A good person speaks with wisdom,
and he says what is fair.
PSALM 37:30 NCV

To get wisdom is to love oneself;
to keep understanding is to prosper.
PROVERBS 19:8 NRSV

Heavenly Father:

You said that wisdom is more precious than gems, and I know that's the truth. What I need right now is Your wisdom in interacting with my children. I've noticed lately that I snap at them after I've had a long day, and I have not been considerate of their feelings. That has engendered strife and has prevented our home from being the safe haven that we all need.

I know the changes must begin with me, and I'm ready to make them. Help me to be respectful of my children, to think before I speak, to put myself in their shoes and see situations through their eyes. Help them and me to always strive to be kind and loving with our words and actions. As we give Your wisdom first place, I'm confident we will reap the peaceful home and relationships that all of us desire.

Amen.

WISDOM IS CONSIDERATE

All moms agree that wisdom is essential in raising children. The scriptures teach that there are two distinct varieties: spiritual and unspiritual. (See James 3:13-18.) Unspiritual wisdom harbors bitterness, envy, and selfish ambition in the heart.

"What's up with you, Mom?" fifteen-year-old Danny asked, looking up when the door slammed.

"Didn't you hear me blow the horn?" Rachel snapped back.

"I guess the television is a little loud, huh?"

"Just bring in the rest of the groceries. I'm tired," she said as she tossed her keys loudly onto the counter.

"Mom, can it wait two minutes? This is the championship game and State's got the ball."

"I don't care who has what. I had to give up my girls' night out last night because of your practice. Get the groceries like I said."

Spiritual wisdom, on the other hand, fills the heart with discernment and understanding.

"Hi, honey!" Melinda said as she walked in, arms laden with groceries.

"Oh hi, Mom," Greg sat forward on the couch, eyes glued to the television. "Why didn't you honk?"

Having honked three times, Melinda grinned to herself. "Important game?"

"Championship. State's got the ball. Give me just a minute, and it'll be over."

"Don't worry about it. You're my son, not my errand boy!"

Greg stood up, still watching the screen. He reached to unburden his mom's arms. "Mom, seriously, let me get the rest."

"Thanks, Son," Melinda stood on tiptoe to kiss his cheek. "You're my hero."

Suffice it to say: There are two kinds of wisdom—selfish and unselfish.

My Daughter,

You are right to desire wisdom to dictate your interactions with your children. My wisdom is peace-loving, considerate, full of mercy, and good fruit. These are the attributes that will make your house a home, the safe haven you desire it to be.

You are the one who sets the emotional and spiritual tone for your family. Strive to be tactful with your words and body language. Send signals that say, "I care about what is going on in your life, and I have your best interest at heart." Become sensitive to timing. Test the emotional temperature of your home and adapt accordingly. When everyone is hungry or tired, that is not the time to confront difficult issues.

Wisdom is soft-spoken and brings openness to most situations. As you give it first place, your children will usually follow your lead.

Your loving Father

Work

In all the work you are doing, work the best you can.
Work as if you were doing it for the Lord, not for people.
Remember that you will receive your reward from the Lord,
which he promised to his people. You are serving the Lord Christ.

COLOSSIANS 3:23-24 NCV

Do your work with enthusiasm. Work as if you were serving the
Lord, not as if you were serving only men and women.

EPHESIANS 6:7 NCV

My life is worth nothing unless I use it for doing
the work assigned me by the Lord Jesus.

ACTS 20:24 NLT

To enjoy your work and to accept your lot in life—that is indeed a
gift from God. The person who does that will not need to look back
with sorrow on his past, for God gives him joy.

ECCLESIASTES 5:19-20 TLB

When you eat the labor of your hands,
you shall be happy, and it shall be well with you.

PSALM 128:2 NKJV

WHAT'S WORK?

Renee dropped into an overstuffed armchair where her six-year-old son Tommy was watching his afternoon adventure show.

"I'm tired," Renee said.

"What you been doin'?" six-year-old Tommy asked.

"Working," she sighed, wiping her forehead.

"When I grow up, I'm gonna work," Tommy said.

"What are you going to do?" she asked.

"I'm going to make heads roll," he said in a self-assured tone.

A wide grin broke out on Renee's face. "And who do you know that makes heads roll?"

"Daddy," he glanced at her with a serious look on his face.

"What do you think Daddy does when he makes heads roll?"

"I don't know, but he does it all the time."

"Well, what if you end up doing the kind of work Mommy does instead?"

"That's not work," he looked tickled at her suggesting it.

"Who told you that?"

"Daddy!"

Thirty minutes passed, and Tommy's dad walked through the door. "Hey Trooper," he bellowed.

Tommy ran into his arms, beaming. "Hey, Dad!" he shouted.

"Where's Mommy?"

"She's in the shower. She said to tell you she's getting ready for work."

"What?" Russ was confused. "Where is she going to work?"

"At your office, Dad," he replied.

"What makes you think that?" Russ was frowning.

"'Cause she said when you get home, it'll be her turn to make some heads roll!"

Teach your children to have regard for every honorable occupation, regardless of how little or how much they understand it.

Youth

You who are young, make the most of your youth.
Relish your youthful vigor.
ECCLESIASTES 11:9 MSG

Satisfy us in our earliest youth with your lovingkindness,
giving us constant joy to the end of our lives.
PSALM 90:14 TLB

He fills my life with good things!
My youth is renewed like the eagle's!
PSALM 103:5 TLB

From my earliest youth I have tried to obey you;
your Word has been my comfort.
PSALM 119:52 TLB

A wise youth works hard all summer; a youth who sleeps away the
hour of opportunity brings shame.
PROVERBS 10:5 NLT

A wise youth accepts his father's rebuke;
a young mocker doesn't.
PROVERBS 13:1 TLB

LOOKING UP TO YOUTH

Only six books in the Bible are addressed to individuals: the gospel of Luke and the book of Acts were written to a man named Theophilus; Timothy was the recipient of two of the remaining four documents.

Timothy was held in high regard among his community and chosen by Paul as a partner in his missionary pursuits. His friendship with the great apostle became a mainstay in Paul's life and ministry. Entrusting great responsibility to Timothy, Paul often left him behind to finish a task or sent him ahead to encourage the faith of the believers. Paul considered him so astute that he refers to him as his son in the faith. Timothy remained faithful to Paul during his missionary travels, his frequent persecutions, and his imprisonment.

Paul's confidence in Timothy proved his comrade was a man of great character. He was sensitive, affectionate, dependable, and loyal. Paul told one group of believers that he hoped to send Timothy to them because he had no one like him who took a genuine interest in the welfare of others.

This is all amazing commentary concerning the man named Timothy, yet Paul revealed another very significant thing when he wrote, "Don't let anyone look down on you because you are young."

Timothy was a youth, yet his witness to others was astonishingly powerful. Where did it begin? According to the Scriptures, it began with his mother . . . and with her mother. Paul wrote that it was a living faith "which first lived in . . . your mother Eunice and . . . now lives in you also" (2 Timothy 1:5).

A mother's godly influence upon the young should never be underestimated.

TOPICAL INDEX